The Country of the Blind

AMERICAN UNIVERSITY STUDIES

SERIES XXVI
THEATRE ARTS

VOL. 33

This book is a volume in a Peter Lang monograph series.
Every volume is peer reviewed and meets
the highest quality standards for content and production.

PETER LANG
New York • Bern • Frankfurt • Berlin
Brussels • Vienna • Oxford • Warsaw

Burton Blistein

The Country of the Blind

A New Interpretation of the Plays of Henrik Ibsen

PETER LANG
New York • Bern • Frankfurt • Berlin
Brussels • Vienna • Oxford • Warsaw

Library of Congress Cataloging-in-Publication Data

Names: Blistein, Burton, author.
Title: The country of the blind: a new interpretation
of the plays of Henrik Ibsen / Burton Blistein.
Description: New York: Peter Lang, 2018.
Series: American university studies XXVI: Theatre arts; vol. 33 | ISSN 0899-9880
Includes bibliographical references.
Identifiers: LCCN 2017039773 | ISBN 978-1-4331-4229-1 (hardback: alk. paper)
ISBN 978-1-4331-4355-7 (epdf) | ISBN 978-1-4331-4356-4 (epub)
ISBN 978-1-4331-4357-1 (mobi)
Subjects: LCSH: Ibsen, Henrik, 1828–1906—Criticism and interpretation.
Classification: LCC PT8895 .B55 2018 | DDC 839.822/6—dc23
LC record available at https://lccn.loc.gov/2017039773
DOI 10.3726/b13054

Bibliographic information published by **Die Deutsche Nationalbibliothek.**
Die Deutsche Nationalbibliothek lists this publication in the "Deutsche Nationalbibliografie"; detailed bibliographic data are available on the Internet at http://dnb.d-nb.de/.

The paper in this book meets the guidelines for permanence and durability of the Committee on Production Guidelines for Book Longevity of the Council of Library Resources.

Printed in Germany

For Brigitte Savage who was, and is, indispensable

"What is truth? said jesting Pilate, and would not stay for an answer. … Doth any man doubt, that if there were taken out of men's minds, vain opinions, flattering hopes, false valuations, imaginations as one would, and the like, but it would leave the minds, of a number of men, poor shrunken things, full of melancholy and indisposition, and unpleasing to themselves?"

—Francis Bacon, "Of Truth."

CONTENTS

Preface xi

Chapter 1. Alternative Realities in *Ghosts* 1
Chapter 2. Who Is Ibsen's Enemy of the People? 27
Chapter 3. De Profundis 49
Chapter 4. Hedda's Revenge 81
Chapter 5. The Master Builder 101

Select Bibliography 143

PREFACE

The following essays deal with an aspect of Ibsen's plays frequently noted but rarely given the *sustained* attention, in English, it deserves: the reluctance or inability of his protagonists to confront unpleasant truths about themselves and their consequent attempts to conceal those truths from themselves and from others. His characters grope for the ideal, for happiness, for truth, or for supremacy as the blind might for light, with as little chance of success; hence the title of my book. Ibsen is of course not the only dramatist about whom this might be said. But in the dramas we shall consider the interactions of the various conscious and unconscious avoidances and subterfuges evince a complexity that is unique.

Ibsen employs this ubiquitous human failing much as a great composer might the simple motif that forms the basis for increasingly intricate and innovative variations. The consequence, in the plays considered, is that his personae are not what they appear to be. We shall observe that Helen Alving is not an heroic figure who has sacrificed all for her beloved son; that the "virtuous" Parson Manders may in fact be the father of Oswald; that neither Gregers Werle nor Dr. Thomas Stockmann are the idealists they profess to be; that Halvard Solness and Hedda Gabler are the very antithesis of the persons they imagine themselves. This gulf between appearance and reality is evident even in the case of secondary agents, confirming the supposition that Ibsen believed self-deception inseparable from the human condition.

There are obvious implications for production. It will clearly make a difference if the director and/or actor regards Thomas Stockmann as an idealist committed to Truth at any cost, or as what he actually is—a consummate egotist engaged in a battle for supremacy with his equally egocentric brother. In this connection it is important to note that Ibsen's settings and stage directions, which frequently have symbolic significance, are an integral part of the dramatic structure. They cannot be substantially altered without affecting the intended meaning.

There are implications for interpretation as well. Ibsen's inferred and suppressed meanings constitute a complex web of relationships that can only be adequately revealed through close analysis of the words and actions of his characters, minor as well as major. To omit any component of this complex is to distort and misrepresent the whole.

We have been given several Ibsens over the years: "the realist, the iconoclast, the successful or failed idealist, the poet, the psychologist, the romantic, the antiromantic."[1] Those various reincarnations required different approaches to the interpretation of Ibsen's works. For the most part, however, certain assumptions persisted throughout. These were: that we could rely upon the known facts of Ibsen's life as aids in interpretation; Ibsen was then frequently identified with certain of his protagonists; that, as a rule we could accept his protagonists' words, in particular their self-evaluations, as truthful; and that Ibsen meant by "realism" chiefly modifications or innovations in setting, stagecraft and language.

The controversies that still surround some of the works with which this book deals—*Ghosts*, *The Wild Duck*, *Hedda Gabler*, and *The Master Builder*—testify to the inadequacy of those assumptions. The remaining play, *An Enemy of the People*, is relatively straightforward. It has nonetheless often been misinterpreted because of the identification of Dr. Thomas Stockmann with Henrik Ibsen. That has frequently been the fate of other "problem" plays. An author concerned with issues of permanent interest was thereby transformed into one no longer entirely relevant with the amelioration or resolution of the "problems" which, it was assumed, preoccupied him. Some who admired Ibsen, such as the playwright Arthur Miller, felt obliged to bring him up to date by modifying the text, corrupting and vitiating the original.

Such difficulties can in part be traced to a misconception of what Ibsen meant by "realism," and to a consequent failure to perceive apparent inconsistencies and ambiguities as evidence of unifying, intelligible dramatic schemas.

It is clear that Ibsen strove for realism, as usually understood, in the later plays. "Do we not know that Ibsen repeatedly spoke of his main purpose in writing dramatic dialogue as being to make it 'completely faithful and realistic?' 'The effect of the play,' he writes to the first Swedish producer of *Ghosts*, apropos of the translation of the dialogue, 'depends to a large extent on the audience imagining it is sitting and listening and watching something actually going on in real life.'"[2] That illusion was essential if Ibsen was to depict characters that existed independently, apart from their creator and the audience, or, in John Northam's words "to emphasize the real existence of creatures as real people."[3] Hence the care he took in providing his personae with a history:

> So intimate had Ibsen become with Nora while at work on a *A Doll's House* that when John Paulson asked him why she was called Nora, Ibsen replied in a matter-of-fact tone 'She was really called Leonora, you know, but everyone called her Nora, since she was the spoilt child of the family.' … Once he suddenly remarked to his wife: 'Now I have seen Nora. She came right up to me and put her hand on my shoulder.' 'How was she dressed?' asked his wife. 'She had on a simple blue cotton dress,' he replied without hesitation.[4]

When *Ghosts* first appeared Ibsen was charged with advocating incest and euthanasia of the unfit.[5] He strenuously objected: "I write a play with five characters and they insist on putting in a sixth—namely Ibsen."[6] "They endeavor to make me responsible for the opinions which certain of the personages of my drama express. And yet there is not in the whole book a single opinion, a single utterance, which can be laid to the account of the author."[7]

Ibsen naturally drew upon his own experience when he created his extraordinary personae. To that extent they resemble him. But they are not to be confused with the author, just as we are not to be confused with friends with whom we share certain confidences and opinions. And when he speaks of such resemblances he is careful to attribute them to beings that exist independently and are not mere "mouthpieces" of their creator. Of Dr. Stockmann, typically regarded as such a surrogate, Ibsen said:

> "Dr. Stockmann and I get along so splendidly with one another; we are so much in agreement on many things; but the Doctor is more muddle-headed than I am, and he has besides several other peculiarities which have the effect that people will tolerate hearing from his mouth various things that they perhaps would not have accepted nearly as well if they had been said by me." Years later "Ibsen is said to have told a German friend, after seeing a production of *An Enemy of the People* in Berlin, that Dr. Stockmann 'ist zum Teil ein grotesker Bursche und ein Strudelkopf' ('is to some extent a grotesque kid and a hothead')."[8]

Such remarks are cited by some as evidence that certain characters are "Ibsen disguised." In fact they reveal that Ibsen thought of his creations as separate beings with whom he agreed about some matters, disagreed about others, and criticized when appropriate. That independence was necessary to facilitate "realism" of a very different sort. Like their flesh and blood brethren his protagonists harbor undisclosed thoughts, agendas, desires, which are often the result of experiences predating their appearance on stage. As Daniel Haakonsen perceptively notes:

> [T]here is hardly a single major character in Ibsen's realistic plays who does not lead a secret existence in addition to the one portrayed on the stage. Most of his characters cover over parts of their past history and their present condition by means of pretense and by withholding information. They allow significant causes or events to remain in either semi- or complete obscurity.[9]

It is not unusual for authors to regard their creations as independent, living entities. However, in Ibsen's dramas that independence is extreme. Many of his protagonists, unwilling to confront their shortcomings, deceive not only their associates but themselves. To their conscious or semi-conscious prejudices intentions and practices we must add their unconscious or suppressed impulses. The result is a dramatic structure of extraordinary complexity and depth.

In the plays we shall consider none of the participants can be relied upon for a truthful or accurate assessment. They prefer to think the truth what they would have it rather than what it is. They believe their actions justified and themselves honest even when this is demonstrably false. They are in effect descendants of Peer Gynt, "the embodiment of … compromise, hypocrisy, irresponsibility, and self-delusion."[10] The drama as a whole consists of a complex of stratagems devised by the participants to forestall self-knowledge and to conceal from others the truths they reject. The consequence is that there are no "heroes" or social reformers. They only appear to be such.

The protagonist's stratagems necessarily interact, forbidding each knowledge of each and all knowledge of the meaning of external circumstance. They are, and they remain, ignorant of their own nature, and of the character of their closest associates. None can ever awaken from the dream to which each has contributed. All are forever imprisoned in the maze they have jointly fashioned. Ibsen's "realism"—for which the superficial likeness to "real life" or mimesis as usually understood is a necessary preliminary—calls into question the very meaning of "reality" and "truth." It becomes whatever his protagonists refuse to acknowledge; and that varies from person to person and from moment to moment.

The falsehoods, "life-lies" or "dreams" in which they consciously believe are as a rule the antithesis of their unconscious, suppressed, unacknowledged impulses, fears and desires. There is always the potential for inner, self-destructive conflict between the corrupt, defective actual self, and the perfected imagined, illusory self, and so always the necessity for self-deception. In *that* unconscious, amidst the "facts" one prefers to ignore, lurks the conviction one is in actuality another, very different, decidedly unpleasant individual. This alter ego always threatens to become manifest, and must be actively, continuously, concealed from oneself and one's associates.

Amidst such shifting sands, the protagonists' dreams, longings, ideals necessarily lack a "firm foundation." Success—if one can call it that—is reserved for the few who, like Hilde Wangel, are *completely* immersed in the dream.

Such dramas will necessarily be full of apparent inconsistencies and unresolved issues resulting from equivocation, concealed motives, and the like. The participants will disagree in their account of events, contradict themselves, offer only partial explanations of their actions, refuse to speak about certain issues, and so forth. To grasp the meaning of the whole we must compare their stated intentions with their actions at any given moment and at successive moments, and their different interpretations of the same events. The tension between the immediate effect of the staged play and its meaning upon reflection and analysis gives to the whole a shifting, ambiguous character somewhat akin to the optical illusion known as a Necker Cube, which appears to alternately advance and recede as one views it. In consequence, "the real meaning of Ibsen's plays cannot be comprehended by a theatre audience: 'Hidden from even the most perceptive theatergoers, this meaning exists only for the reader, who can leaf back through the pages, read again, and thereby disrupt the passage of time.'"[11]

On a number of occasions I refer to the "devil" or "devils" that appear in these plays. They are not to be thought of as entities with horns, tails and pitchforks. They are rather Ibsen's way of using common speech ("devil take it," "what the devil") to refer to pervasive, enigmatic evil. The Father of Lies, a sobriquet sometimes applied to the devil (v. John 8:44), refers to the dominant role of self-deceit and the deception of others. Metaphorically, He rules this cosmos.

Brief references in this text to other authors who have written on Ibsen are included simply to highlight what I perceive to be distinctive features of my own interpretation. They should not be regarded as criticism or evaluation of those works in their entirety.

This book was written for the general reader and for companies contemplating production of the plays discussed as well as for scholars—not necessarily scholars fluent in Norwegian, but interested in Ibsen. Use of translations and citations from studies in English seemed therefore appropriate. I have cited from alternative translations and from the Norwegian in those few cases where translations seemed to me problematic.

Notes

1. Charles R. Lyons, *Critical Essays*, 4.
2. Inga-Stina Ewbank, "Ibsen's Dramatic Language as a Link between his 'Realism' and His 'Symbolism'" in Lyons, *Critical Essays*, 69.
3. John Northam, "Ibsen's Dramatic Method" in McFarlane, *Henrik Ibsen: A Critical Anthology*, 269.
4. P. F. D. Tennant, "Ibsen's Dramatic Technique" in McFarlane, *Henrik Ibsen: A Critical Anthology*, 251.
5. Hermann J. Weigand, *Modern Ibsen*, 98.
6. Henrik Ibsen in McFarlane, *Henrik Ibsen: A Critical Anthology*, 93.
7. Hermann J. Weigand, *Modern Ibsen*, 98.
8. Thomas F. Van Laan, "Generic Complexity," 102.
9. Daniel Haakonsen, "'The Play-within-the-Play' in Ibsen's Realistic Drama," in Lyons, *Critical Essays*, 217.
10. Robert Brustein, "Ibsen and Revolt," 133.
11. Age Henriksen cited by Daniel Haakonsen, "The Play-within," in Lyons, *Critical Essays*, 216.

References

All parenthetical page citations in this text are from *Eleven Plays of Henrik Ibsen*, ed. B. A. Cerf, D. S. Klopfer. New York: *The Modern Library*, 1935. Translators not given but those of plays discussed in this volume appear to be R. Farquharson Sharp (*Ghosts*, *An Enemy of the People*), Edmund Gosse and William Archer (*The Master Builder*, *Hedda Gabler*), and William Archer (*The Wild Duck*). I found those older translations satisfactory for my purposes. In the few cases where translation appeared to be an issue I have appended parallel citations from *The Oxford Ibsen*, 8 vols. London: Oxford University Press, 1962.

Brustein, Robert. "Ibsen and Revolt." *The Tulane Review* 7, no. 1 (Autumn 1962): 113–154.

Lyons, Charles R., ed. *Critical Essays on Henrik Ibsen*. Boston: G. K. Hall & Co., 1987.

McFarlane, James, ed. *Henrik Ibsen: A Critical Anthology*. Harmondsworth, Middlesex, England: Penguin Books, 1970.

Van Laan, Thomas F. "Generic Complexity in Ibsen's 'An Enemy of the People.'" *Comparative Drama* 20, no. 2 (Summer 1986): 95–114.

Weigand, Hermann J. *The Modern Ibsen*. New York: Henry Holt & Co., 1925.

· 1 ·

ALTERNATIVE REALITIES IN *GHOSTS*

Prefatory

It is evident that light is associated with the revelation of truth in *Ghosts*, and darkness with its antithesis, the hidden, the shameful, the surreptitious. As Helene Alving aptly remarks: "we are so miserably afraid of the light, all of us" (134). Yet the drama concludes with Oswald, who has apparently learned the truth from his mother concerning his inherited disease, asking her for the "sun" or in effect for the truth. Are we to attribute this symbolic *non sequitur* at the climactic moment simply to syphilitic induced blindness and dementia, or does Oswald's complaint conceal a deeper meaning?

There are many such unresolved issues in the drama. The very structure of Ibsen's language with its frequent unfinished exchanges is one consequence. The play ends with an incomplete remark signaling indecision. Will Helene decide to give her son the deadly morphia or not? This is but one of many possible alternative realities. Is the rain God's gift as Engstrand claims, or, as Regine insists, is it the devil's work? More broadly, is this an intrinsically evil cosmos, one in which evil is punished by a wise and benevolent God, or is it neither? Is Oswald delighted to be home as he first says or in despair as he later maintains? Does he love his mother or has long absence made him indifferent? Did Oswald contract his disease from his father or in Paris? If the latter, can his account of his life there be trusted? Was his father an unregenerate rogue or one in whom the love of life was crushed by an overly moralistic spouse? Helene gives different accounts at different times to Manders and to Oswald. Is the apparently healthy Regine disease free, or will she, too, eventually succumb to inherited disease? If Regine is truly healthy can the Captain have had syphilis? Did Manders start the Orphanage fire, or did Engstrand in order to accuse Manders of it and so gain the upper hand? If the Captain was in fact syphilitic, then Mrs. Alving, who tended him until his death, must be familiar with its symptoms. Why, then, is she shocked to learn of Oswald's prognosis after she implies his illness could very well have been inherited? ("Your father was a lost ["broken," "ravaged"] man before ever you were born" [164].) Why does she say it is "impossible" for him to be afflicted and make light of its certain consequences? Does she believe she has a legitimate reason, or is it simply a mother's natural reluctance to confront a painful truth about her son? What is the significance of the pipe-smoking incident? Was the Captain trying to corrupt the young Oswald, instill in him abhorrence for tobacco, or pass on to him syphilis via his oral lesions? If the first or the last alternative, why such animosity toward one's own offspring? Helene's and Manders' accounts of their past relationship differ significantly. She recalls much greater intimacy than he. Who is correct?

Eric Bentley notes that for many this multiplicity of possibilities is an insuperable aesthetic defect: "A picture composed of such unclear details can only come together in our minds as a fog."[1] Max Nordau attributes it to mental incompetence, claiming that in Ibsen's work, "Everything floats and undulates, nebulous and amorphous, such as we are accustomed to see in weak-brained degenerates."[2]

Such criticisms misconstrue Ibsen's unique creation. The landmarks implied by the terms "reality" and "truth" elude us in *Ghosts*; and that is precisely the effect Ibsen intended. The author deliberately presents us with alternative realities and denies us the satisfaction of preferring one to the other. His protagonists consciously inhabit a secondary, superficial reality. This is the reality evident from a cursory reading and in the theater. Their unconscious and concealed motives and desires constitute the primary, fundamental reality. This is the reality that emerges from careful scrutiny of the written text. It is accessible only through the secondary reality and hence necessarily remains uncertain, notwithstanding its importance. The difficulty of deciding among alternatives is rooted in the attempts of Ibsen's characters to conceal what they and their peers perceive as sinful, shameful, illegitimate or criminal behavior. The result is a cosmos in which truth is elusive and ultimately unattainable—for the reader or spectator as well as for the protagonists. The blind Oswald's final request for the "sun" symbolic of truth, which cannot be granted, perfectly sums up the whole.

Ibsen's Orphanage—regarded as the refuge not only of children whose parents are deceased but also of the illegitimate whose parents refuse to acknowledge them—embodies the universal impulse to bury, to conceal and so avoid responsibility for one's wrongs. Those presumably "dead" remnants of the past return in this drama like ghosts to plague the living. Consistent with this there are two basic plot progressions—one towards consecration of the Orphanage and the concealment of wrongdoing, another towards the revelation of what it was created to conceal. The first ends in flames that annihilate the institution symbolic of hidden shame and corruption; the second ends not in the revelation of truth as we are led to expect, but in ambiguity and indecision.

For Hermann Weigand the ghosts of *Ghosts* are, in part, "[A]ncient, outworn views and notions [which] continue to spook in the feelings of the individual, long after their rational underpinning has fallen."[3] And, to be sure, many of the issues raised by the drama are clearly the consequences of a repressive social order that was vanishing in Ibsen's day and no longer exists. If we believe this the *raison d'être* of the play, Ibsen figures as a social critic whose time has passed. Infidelity, prostitution, alcoholism, and sexually transmitted disease are now openly discussed. Syphilis responds to antibiotics. Today, one might argue, the ending of *Ghosts* would have to be rewritten.

Such assessments assume a radical discontinuity between the earlier overtly symbolic and the later "realistic" dramas. But in fact the Ibsen of *Peer Gynt* and *Brand*, preoccupied with fundamental, timeless issues, did not vanish with the introduction of topical subject matter. Rather, the latter became for him a means to cloak those same issues in realistic dress.

To cite but one example: Captain Alving's illness is not specified. Those who regard Ibsen as a social critic see this as the result of societal repression: syphilis was a forbidden topic and hence unmentionable. In fact Oswald's illness is symbolic for the playwright of an "illness" that afflicts all of mankind, an illness inherited from our first parents and passed down through the generations, and so conveniently represented by syphilis. Had Ibsen identified syphilis as such his larger meaning might have been obscured. As Hugh Kenner observes, "champion and detractor alike have failed to notice that [Ibsen] was employing mental imbalance of venereal origin as a relevant metaphor for original sin," and that we have in *Ghosts* "a colossal catastrophe motivated by the nemesis of hidden sins."[4] Syphilis frequently masquerades as other illnesses, "leading one nineteenth-century clinician, Jonathan Hutchinson, to dub it the 'Great Imitator.'"[5] It is thus the perfect engine of retribution in a society committed to deceit or masquerade. For similar reasons the illness in *Enemy of the People*, which was probably cholera, is not specified. It represents the moral pollution and corruption rampant not only in that population but in mankind at large; and those will persist whether or not science eventually finds a cure for the physical ailment. The nineteenth century was a time of rapid advances in medicine. Ibsen, trained as a pharmacist, wisely avoided the specificity that would have obscured his meaning and might in future have made his dramas obsolete.

It would therefore be wrong to regard *Ghosts* as a plea for the extermination of outmoded beliefs and prejudices. Oswald and Helene, who advocate this, are ruined. And they are, as I hope to demonstrate, precisely because of flaws inseparable from their humanity. Even if we assume that the captain is responsible for Oswald's tragedy—which is not certain—profligacy such as his, and the impulse to conceal or "repress" painful truths are as common today as they were in the past. The original title of *Ghosts*, *Gengangere*, signifies "those who return." And in fact its subject is those human failings that endure. Their consequences, like revenants, invariably "return" to plague one. That fate awaits nearly all in Ibsen's drama despite their attempts to elude it.

In this connection it is important to note that Helene is not to be regarded as a Nora Helmer *manqué* who might have avoided disaster had she acted differently. She abandoned her husband after one year of marriage and returned to him only after she was rejected by the man she loved. After learning of Alving's affair with their servant, Joanna, she ended his public profligacy. "I took the upper hand in the house, absolutely—both with him and all the others. … It was then that Oswald was sent away. He was about seven then …" (124). (McFarlane: "So I took control in the house … complete control … over him and everything else.") She alone managed Alving's estate, so successfully that she became independently wealthy. She sent her son away when he was seven to remove him from the captain. Thereafter he had no contact with Alving. As she remarks, speaking specifically of Alving's estate but implying far more, Oswald was to "inherit" everything from her (126, 127). She failed to accomplish this because of the devious and corrupt behavior of others and her own fear of exposure. Her experience does not demonstrate what would have happened to Nora had she not left her husband, but rather the inevitable limitations imposed by the human condition upon even the most talented and determined of women.

It is unlikely that, as Alexis Solsoki argues, "disease destroys the Alving family not because of the father's transgressions, but because of the mother's moral continence."[6] If Helene denied Alving his conjugal rights it was almost certainly because she believed him already infected, and did not want to pass on his sickness to any offspring. Joan Templeton argues, rightly I think, that to condemn Helene "does enormous injustice to the play. For what it ignores is the indisputable fact that Helene Alving loved another man; so much so that she committed the unspeakable act of leaving her husband for him. It would thus seem both preposterous and cruel to demand that she feel passion for her husband." She adds: "no matter how 'joyful' Mrs. Alving had made her husband's home, there is absolutely nothing to suggest Oswald's condition would have changed a whit. The argument that the captain caught the disease after she had rejected him and that she is therefore responsible is not only a fallacious post hoc argument in itself but one impossible to maintain on any textual grounds whatsoever."[7]

Act I

As in Ibsen's dramas generally, the staging is crucial. In *Ghosts*, where truth is concealed and the possibility of knowing or not knowing therefore of great moment, we have a centrally located room with doors opening on two sides. It provides opportunity for anyone in or near it—watering the plants in the conservatory for example, or on the stairs leading to the kitchen, or at the central table or the work table—to overhear conversations elsewhere. Helene points out they are inaudible if the peripheral doors are closed; but when voices are raised that may not be true; and, as we later learn, the doors are not always closed. Two of the most critical conversations *are* overheard by her—the first when the Captain accosts Joanna, the second when his "ghost," Oswald, accosts her daughter, Regine. Helene's "stifled cry" (143) upon discovering Oswald in the adjacent dining room after what she thought was a private conversation with Manders indicates concern about such revelations. Ibsen's society is populated by individuals who prefer to keep their dirty secrets secret, their "ghosts" in the grave as it were, but can never be sure they have succeeded.

Joanna waited upon the Alvings at Rosenvold. Like Regine, she would often have had occasion to visit the conservatory or use the kitchen stairs and perhaps the work table. She could have overheard conversations that revealed family secrets and passed them on to Engstrand after their marriage. As we shall note, this may in part explain Engstrand's hold over the parson.

The conservatory within, the incessant rain without, the act of watering the conservatory plants, which Regine has just completed, are all symbolic. In Ibsen's day syphilis was erroneously thought to be transmitted by the semen of the male. "Ibsen believed, like most in his day, that syphilis was hereditary, and that Oswald got it from his father at conception."[8] And so one can compare fatality in this play to the growth or blossoming of a seed planted long ago. It is in effect watered by the rain that obscures the sun, emblem of the truth—(for this "growth" is fostered by the suppression of truth)—which induces in Oswald despair that accelerates his decline, appropriately terminating in blindness signifying utter ignorance of the truth. At Rosenvold, the center and focal point of deception past and present, there is "Never a ray of sunshine." Oswald cannot "remember ever having seen the sun shine once" when he was at home (148). Shortly before his collapse he exits into the rain without his hat. Ibsen twice refers to this (156, 157) to emphasize the relationship between Oswald's mind, gradually succumbing to moral as well as physical corruption, and the rain symbolic of the deception responsible for this insidious progression.

By contrast, within Rosenvold all appears serene. The conservatory, seemingly isolated from the rain and gloom without, apparently subject to human control, represents a world in which beauty is cultivated. It is the world Ibsen associates with the "joy of life," the world depicted in Oswald's paintings: "There is light there, and sunshine, and a holiday feeling—and people's faces beaming with happiness" (154). This is the world that the "canker" within the worm eaten ("*vermoulu*") Oswald feeds upon and destroys, as the worm destroys the plant (147). *Ghosts* reveals it to be as illusory, as artificial and transitory as the world depicted in Oswald's paintings. That revelation is initiated now by Engstrand, who enters, bringing with him the rain symbolic of destructive deceit:

Regine (below her breath) [to Engstrand].	What is it you want? Stay where you are. The rain is dripping off you.
Engstrand.	God's good rain, my girl.
Regine.	The Devil's own rain, that's what it is! (95)

And, indeed, is the pernicious destructive growth this rain promotes the consequence of a world in which wrong is justly punished, of one intrinsically evil, or of indifferent Darwinian nature? Is it ruled by God, by the Devil, or by neither?

Ibsen does not resolve this. *Ghosts* suggests that the second alternative is more plausible; but one cannot be certain. Regine refers to Engstrand's withered leg as "*Pied de mouton*" (98). Both attributes signify descent from the Adversary, Father of Lies, traditionally lame and cloven-hoofed. His "offspring," Engstrand, appears to triumph in the end. He "converts" Manders, ostensible paragon of morality, to his duplicitous ways. The two leave together virtually, or actually, arm in arm. Engstrand's Sailors' Home, symbol and center of corruption, will supplant the Orphanage dedicated to God.

But the Orphanage was established to conceal evil. Its destruction is thus justified. And Manders' new intimacy with Engstrand, who has blackmailed him, marks him indelibly as the hypocrite he always was. One foresees a most unpleasant future for the parson, given his obsessive fear of exposure and the likelihood of future impositions by Engstrand, who now controls him. With respect to the nature of this cosmos, Ibsen's ending raises more questions than it answers.

Engstrand's occupation tells us he is not your typical devil. Like Christ, also a carpenter, he assumes the burden of other's sins. However, his purpose is not to liberate them from sin but to commit them to it irrevocably. He controls his victims—Joanna, Manders, the captain and Helene—by taking responsibility for their wrongs.

Regine, who speaks first in the play, immediately introduces the element of subterfuge, of hidden motives and objectives. She tells Engstrand that "*Pied de mouton*" is English to conceal her hopes for a sojourn in Paris with Oswald; and subsequently, unwilling to attribute the "devilish" rain to that source before the parson, tells Manders "It's a splendid rain for the farmers," or, in effect God's rain, evidence of His bounty. She plays up to Manders, ostensibly asking for his assistance in finding employment in town, but actually offering to be his "companion" as her mother was the captain's (104). She hides from Helene, who expects her to work in the Orphanage, her intention to leave Rosenvold, from the parson her intention to leave with Oswald, and from Oswald her solicitation of Manders. Although not Engstrand's daughter she has clearly "inherited" his vices, resembling in that respect the other descendents of Adam who populate *Ghosts*.

For his part, Oswald has "inherited" his father's alcoholism and lasciviousness. He initially conceals those vices just as Regine conceals her ambitious plans, complicating the mix of hidden agendas that constitute this drama. But vices such as Oswald's, which promise success for Engstrand's Sailors' Home, are, like Regine's offer of her body to Manders and to Oswald, common enough. Of themselves they do not signify descent from one's immediate parents, but, as noted, from our first parents after their banishment from the

Garden. The return of the dead and re-enactment of past sins depicted in *Ghosts* are ubiquitous and continuous. Sin is "original" and therefore passed down from generation to generation: "The sins of the fathers are visited on the children" in perpetuity (147). Syphilis, transmitted by the universal, inevitable gratification of desire, conveniently represents this relationship. The disease has a third or "latent" stage, which can last from ten to thirty years. During that "hidden" phase there are no outward signs. It perfectly represents the cosmos of *Ghosts*—outwardly benign because of suppressed or hidden sin, inwardly corrupt and worm-eaten.

Manders' submission to Engstrand is striking. He is clearly capable of condemning those he thinks have done wrong—witnesses his self-righteous critique of Helene for failing in her roles of wife and mother. Yet, save for a brief interlude, he consistently pardons Engstrand's transgressions. One suspects that Engstrand has some hold over him. And that may indeed be the case; for Manders is the perfect hypocrite, and so vulnerable. In all probability he conceals the truth throughout just as he obviously does at the end.

To understand him we must assume that his words typically cloak his actual beliefs and intentions. He is obviously interested in Regine, now blossoming into womanhood, yet in conversation with Helene he professes ignorance of such "things" (135). When Regine kneels before him to place a footstool, and—given the various comments praising her appearance, and her intention to seduce Oswald or, if that proves impossible, to interest Manders—probably wearing a dress as revealing as custom and station will allow, she draws his gaze. "I certainly think you have grown since I saw you last," he says (102). He addresses her as "my dear Regine …," "my dear good child" when in effect she offer herself to him (104). Although Manders abruptly terminates this encounter, Regine senses his preoccupation with her person saying later "Mr. Manders takes an interest in me, I know" (166). Regine is equally duplicitous. She condemns Engstrand for emphasizing her mother's moral "flexibility" but is quite willing to follow in her footsteps. She hopes to have Manders employ her with the prospect of replicating, ghost-like, her mother's intimacy with Alving should the promised trip to Paris not materialize.

This sensual interlude is immediately followed by Manders' silent condemnation of the "abominable, subversive, free thinking literature" lying about (104, 134). Such hypocrisy is characteristic of all protagonists, Engstrand affording the hypocritic "gold standard."

Given his fear of scandal it is admittedly a stretch to assume that Manders would ever consider employing Regine. However, Regine apparently thinks this a possibility, and so it cannot be discounted. Manders must detach Regine from Helene if she is to become a member of his household. Hence, perhaps, his emphasis upon her need to return to Engstrand. He insists that she "go home with" Engstrand even *after* he learns from Helene that Engstrand is not her father and agrees with her that Regine should not, therefore, live with him (155); or he recommends what he must know will be a questionable relationship because, as noted, Engstrand has some hold over him. Whatever his motive or motives, it is clear that this clergyman, who habitually cloaks his misdeeds in sanctimonious sermonizing, is willing to depart from truth, morality, and legality when it suits him. He welcomes Engstrand's acceptance of responsibility for the fire that he, Manders, may have started; yet immediately afterward remarks to Helene, "may the spirit of order and what is lawful speedily enter into this house" (161). (McFarlane: "And may I hope that very soon some sense of order and propriety will find its way into this house.")

Ibsen includes this egregious instance of hypocrisy to signify that Manders cannot be trusted. He is not motivated—as F. W. Kaufmann and others insist—by "absolute moral demands."[9] The evidence contradicts Northam's assertion that Manders is "not … a hypocrite … [but] deeply and sincerely moved … in conventional ways."[10] The parson's thoughts and actions throughout belie his professed beliefs. His protestations of innocence, of ignorance of the darker, subterranean impulses are misleading. We find his like among the "model husbands and fathers" described by Oswald, who condemn "the prevalence of immorality abroad" because "experts in the matter," having themselves deliberately sought out depravity there (117–118). It is therefore quite possible that Engstrand knows of something in Manders' past that the parson does not wish disclosed, and that Manders accommodates him because of this. If this supposition is correct, then Engstrand's blackmail of Manders at the conclusion of *Ghosts* is not unique, but itself a "ghost," a *revenant* from, or recapitulation of, the past.

Helene abandoned her husband for Manders. He still fears the possible repercussions. Participating with her in the Orphanage dedicated to the captain's memory is one way for him to put to rest rumors of their former intimacy. And indeed, as I argue in the following pages, the two may have been intimate. If so, then the parson's involvement in the Orphanage also figures as an attempt to conceal past sins, resembling in that respect Helene's dedication of it to the memory of a supposedly benevolent benefactor who was, according to her, a dissolute rogue. What better obfuscation of the truth than to supervise the construction of a memorial to the man you betrayed?

To the multitude it must appear that Helene and Manders are now, and were in the past, completely innocent. Hence, in part, Manders refusal to spend the night at Rosenvold; his avoidance of Helene's embrace (Regine or Oswald might be watching); his insistence that Helene not insure their enterprise, thus publicly establishing their spiritual credentials, their mutual trust in divine providence; and his reluctance, save during moments of great stress when he forgets himself, to call Helene by her first name or address her as "*Dear* Mrs. Alving"—an adjective he freely bestows upon Regine and Oswald. Given Manders characteristic modes of thinking and acting, his insistence upon propriety and aversion to physical contact suggest the antithesis—namely, that at some point his relationship with Helene was less than respectable, and that he still desires her. Her dead husband perhaps affords some insight into this possibility.

The only specific action of the captain we are told about, the single aspect of the relationship with his father that Oswald recalls, is the incident of the meerschaum pipe. (Oswald: "I never knew anything of my father. I don't remember anything else about him except that he once made me sick" [167]). Manders says, "It was an extremely odd thing to do." Helene asserts that it did not happen; Oswald only dreamt it, she says (115). But clearly he did not. How are we to explain the captain's "extremely odd" behavior? Why is Helene so anxious to deny that the incident happened? And does Manders—who refused to visit the Alvings after Helene abandoned her husband for him—really think it "odd"?

Helene's desertion of her husband, her refusal to return to him "in spite of his requests and entreaties" (119), her sojourn with Manders, who had been their daily companion, whom she loved before she married Alving (130), and who was obviously in love with her (134) suggest possible answers to these questions.

Helene tells Manders that "after nineteen years of married life" her husband died "just as profligate … as he was before you married us" (123–124). And again: "Do you suppose my husband was any purer, when I went with him to the altar, than Joanna was when Engstrand agreed to marry her?" (130). And again: "I let myself be bound in marriage to a fallen man" (130). She tells Oswald "your father was a lost man before ever you were born" (164; in Norwegian "lost" = "*nebrudt*" or "a *ravaged* man" as by disease). The captain, if syphilitic, was almost certainly so when the title of Chamberlain was bestowed; for it is characteristic of this cosmos that the most attractive and apparently innocent surfaces conceal corruption. Oswald is now 26 or 27

(116). Helene's marriage lasted nineteen years, and it is now precisely ten years since the captain's death (119). Oswald was obviously born early in the marriage—possibly within a year of the time Helene left and returned to her husband after their first year of marriage. Ibsen's chronology allows for the possibility that Manders could have been Oswald's father. (James Joyce suggests this in his poem "Epilogue to Ibsen's 'Ghost's.'"[11]) Had Ibsen made Oswald 25 or younger, which he easily could have done, there would be no question of possible paternity. One must ask, therefore, why *this* chronology? As Haakonsen justly observes in Ibsen's dramas "the more firmly [secrets are] concealed, the more explanatory they are."[12] "Ibsen's 'retrospective technique' does not create its richest effects by the secrets is reveals, but by what it takes care not to reveal and merely lets us suspect—once we are in sympathy with that trend towards ever deeper-lying explanations which it sets moving, and which does not permit a stop to be made at any arbitrary time or any particular point."[13]

Manders' paternity would explain most of the puzzling aspects of this play. More to the present point, like Helene's remark that she married "a fallen man," her assertion that the wealthy, popular Alving, was "a lost [or "ravaged"] man before ever [Oswald] was born" indicates he was probably ill when he married. In view of the then-prevalent notion that syphillis was transmitted by the male, had this woman, so devoted to her son, discovered that the captain was syphilitic, she obviously would have preferred Manders—whom she truly loved and regretted rejecting—to be her child's father. She despised the captain; that was why she left him. He must have perceived her aversion. He surely would have thought his disease and her dislike motives enough for her flight to the parson, especially if she had previously been reluctant to have intercourse with him because of his affliction. She did not return to Alving immediately "in spite of his requests and entreaties." With whom was she staying, if not with Manders? And what might have happened during the interval? Manders ceased his visits thereafter. Could that have been the consequence of a guilty conscience? For whatever reason or reasons, rightly or wrongly, the captain would have had cause to suspect that his wife had been unfaithful during her absence, and that her child, born within a year of her return to him, was not his. It is possible that he perceived or imagined he perceived in Oswald, when he was seven and his features were forming, a certain likeness to the parson. Helene observes that the adult Oswald's mouth resembles a clergyman's, meaning of course Manders' (124).

By the time Oswald was seven, Helene had, by her own account, put an end to her husband's dissolute excursions by threatening to reveal his affair with Joanna. He had become her virtual prisoner. What better revenge than to infect, or sicken, or corrupt the child, whom the captain may have resented, perhaps even hated, via his pipe, and so thwart the plans of an unfaithful, dictatorial spouse?[14] There is malevolence in the words and laughter Oswald recalls: "'Smoke my boy,'" Alving said, "'have a good smoke, boy!' … Then he laughed—such a hearty laugh—" (114). The captain's suspicions would also explain his infrequent contact with Oswald, this incident being, as noted, the only encounter with Alving Oswald remembers.

The captain's enmity, his possible allusion to his wife's infidelity, and the threat of contagion could explain why Helene wept when she happened upon the two, and why, after making every effort to insure that Oswald was not infected at birth, she sent him away from a house she regarded as "polluted." Helene would not want Oswald to know about her desertion of the husband she despised yet praised in her letters to him, or of the captain's tacit accusation of infidelity—which might in future become explicit—that culminated in the incident of the meerschaum pipe, or of his actual parentage. She would have reason to conceal her flight from the marriage she abhorred, and therefore to deny the existence of the incident that suggests it might have happened, as in fact she does. She does not tell Oswald about her abandonment of home and hearth even when she later reveals the "truth" about his father to him.

To this we must add that, save for her deceptive letters, Oswald was raised by Helene as if he were *not* Alving's child. He was not allowed to return to his home "as long as the captain was alive" (125). Helene saw to it that he would not inherit his father's substantial estate. It was invested in the Orphanage. Oswald himself became very nearly an orphan for twelve years—without a father or a mother present. Indeed, he identifies himself with the Orphanage: "Everything will burn. They'll be nothing left to remind people of Father. And here I am burning down too."[15] As Inge-Stina Ewbank remarks, "[Ibsen's] metaphor obviously serves to link the surface with the underlying symbolic structure: through the metaphor we see for a moment Oswald as identified with the Orphanage and both as products of Captain Alving's life—and of Mrs. Alving's gladless "duty to 'cover up.'"[16] If we assume that Manders was in fact Oswald's father the Orphanage figures in part as an offering by Helene to assuage her guilt for denying her son all knowledge of his true parent and to that extent "orphaning" him. If not, then it may express her guilty wish that Manders *had* been his father. Her attribution of the project to an "uneasy" or "guilty" conscience (125) could signify either of those possibilities as well as her stated intention to silence all possible rumors of her husband's profligacy (125).

Weigand, who emphasizes the last, thinks her "guilty conscience" owing to her "intellectual emancipation" in conflict with "the [conservative] habits of a lifetime."[17] That is unlikely. Helene obviously felt no remorse for having abandoned the captain years ago, but only regret for Manders' rejection of her and her resumption of the stifling role of dutiful wife. Her letters to Oswald described not her husband, but a hypothetical, non-existent surrogate who "did so much ... that was good and useful"—perhaps inspired by Helene's equally imaginary conception of the parson.

As noted in the prefatory remarks there are other possible explanations of the meerschaum incident. But Manders' role seems to me the most plausible. The captain was on the spot. He knew Helene and Manders well; he must have sensed his wife's interest in the parson, who visited them daily, and his interest in her; and he was of course aware of his own troubled marital relations. If his suspicions were as I have suggested—and it is hard to justify his abusive treatment of Oswald otherwise—it is *prima facie* evidence that Oswald might indeed be Manders' child.

The Alvings moved from the town to isolated Rosenvold soon after Helene, rejected by Manders, returned to the captain (122). She might have required it as a condition of her return to put some distance between his nightly excursions and the household; perhaps she feared the townspeople would perceive her growing son's resemblance to the parson; or the captain might have insisted upon it to isolate a wife he suspected had been unfaithful. All explanations are plausible. Alving's stratagem—if that's what it was—clearly worked. Manders did not contact or visit them thereafter. Helene was also successful to a degree. Although the captain did not cease his profligate behavior, after they moved to Rosenvold he "indulged it in secret, when he was out of the house" (123), meaning presumably in the town. Apparently Helene did not object to his dissipation as long as it occurred elsewhere. It obviated the need to have intercourse with him. She prohibited his excursions completely only after she learned of Alving's affair with her own servant in her own house (124).

Helene subsequently "took charge" of Alving. Oswald was then about seven (124). By threatening the captain with exposure, blackmailing him just as Engstrand blackmails Manders, she was apparently able to terminate his profligate excursions to the mainland. For eleven years this sick man had to subordinate his wishes to his wife's, becoming a virtual prisoner in his own home. There is, then, an explanation other than the one Helene first offers for his drunken bouts at Rosenvold and what she represents as his maudlin self-pity. Helene became expert at concealment—hiding her husband's progressive degeneration and his indifference to the society that honored him for the good works that were in fact her doing. Her letters to Oswald about a father who did not exist are of a piece with this. She clearly was capable of concealing the truth about Oswald's parentage, if he was in fact illegitimate.

Helene Alving is obviously intelligent and level-headed—she did after all manage her husband's estate successfully for many years. She surely would not have abandoned Alving for Manders had she not believed that Manders reciprocated her affection. She would not have said "Here I am, take me!" if she thought him indifferent (135). An entire, unexpressed history of their relationship informs those few words. The sexual implications are clear and understandable if for a year she had refrained from intercourse with an infected spouse who had made her abysmally unhappy. For more than one reason Helene might have wanted Manders to be the father of her child. In this connection, it is perhaps significant that Helene, who so astutely managed her husband's affairs in the past, surrenders to Manders all control of the captain's estate, making him, with respect to that, a sort of surrogate husband. She attributes this to a wish to end her responsibility for the despised Alving's affairs. But her purpose may also be to remind Manders of his former and current role in her life. Her request that he stay the night, her attempt to embrace him, her evocation of a past when they were close, her misinterpretation of his craven submission to Engstrand as the act of an innocent "big baby," (142) suggest that she probably still loves him. She may have initiated the project of the Orphanage (107) in part to reestablish her former relationship with the parson, who had long avoided her, and to remind him that Oswald was his "orphaned" child. Her remark about their resemblance (see below) would then have special point.

Charles Leland finds evidence in the play that Manders "had known intense sexual love" for Helene Alving, and that their love "involved physical attraction on both sides." He thinks the parson "still deeply in love with Mrs. Alving." In view of this he finds it "hard to fathom" why Manders "for some reason believes that this love is unacceptable" since "by this time Mrs. Alving is a widow for whom the eminently respectable pastor might be a good match."[18] Ten years have elapsed since the captain's death, and so that was long a possibility. The difficulty vanishes if we assume that Manders is Oswald's father and therefore quite possibly the source of his disease. To infect others would obviously incriminate the parson. Fear of this eventuality could account for his prolonged avoidance of physical intimacy, not only with

Helene, but with all women. His celibacy may not indicate impotence, as some think, but rather potency accompanied by the disease symbolic of moral corruption.

After Helene returned to her husband Manders ceased his visits to the Alvings, who had moved to Rosenvold. He did not contact Helene during the captain's lifetime. Hence Manders had no way of knowing whether he was Oswald's father even were that true. He may have stayed away to relieve himself of any possible responsibility for an illegitimate child; to avoid the ire of an angry husband; or to prevent difficult private conversations with Helene concerning their former relationship. He is clearly capable of such cowardice, as we learn from his abject surrender to Engstrand when the latter offers to relieve him of "responsibility" for the Orphanage fire.

We do not know, we cannot know, what came of Helene's and Manders' early "intimacy," if one can call it that. It is clear that, after an unspecified delay, Manders sent Helene back to her husband. We do not know what happened beforehand. Helene consistently refers to the captain as Oswald's father, and Manders never gives the slightest hint of anything irregular in their former relationship. But then he would not do so, nor would she. They, and Oswald, would be ruined by the ensuing scandal should word get out, and Oswald would be furious to learn of his mother's deceit. There are, however indications of Manders' affection for, and unusual interest in, Oswald, whom he treats as a father might his son. He closely followed Oswald's career. He is concerned about his morals as he is not about Engstrand's whose failings he repeatedly excuses. He addresses Oswald familiarly as "Dear Oswald." He condemns Helene for not providing a proper home for Oswald and sending her son away at an early age.

Always conscious of the need to avoid even a hint of scandal, past or present, Manders perceives in Oswald a resemblance to Alving. When Helene observes that, to the contrary, Oswald has a clergyman's mouth—with the clear implication that he might be the parson's son—Manders quickly adds that many of his *colleagues* have such a mouth (114). That absurd reply is almost certainly an attempt to disclaim paternity. In view of Manders' habitual evasiveness it suggests, for this very reason, the possibility of paternity.

Consider also this exchange:

Manders. Can you call it cowardice that you simply did your duty! Have you forgotten that a child should love and honour his father and mother?

Mrs. Alving. Don't let us talk in such general terms. Suppose we say: "Ought Oswald to love and honour Mr. Alving?" (132)

Surely the more obvious and relevant question would be "Ought Oswald to love and honour *his own* father?" with the implication that "Mr. Alving" was not. In sum, one must allow for the possibility that beneath the many partially expressed and concealed relationships of *Ghosts* there may be another, and that the most important, altogether unexpressed save for the trail of "breadcrumbs" Ibsen has left us, namely that Oswald is Manders' son, a fact which Helene has hidden from Manders, heroically assuming all responsibility for her illegitimate offspring who was to derive "everything" from her (126). As noted above, this suggests a still more shocking possibility—that the parson is a syphilitic who as yet exhibits no outward signs of the disease, and that he rather than the Captain infected Oswald. The "virtuous" Manders is obviously morally corrupt. To assign to this hypocrite the affliction symbolic of concealed moral corruption is therefore perfectly appropriate, Ibsen's larger point being that "The price of respectability has been wholesale deceit."[19] Society's very citadels of virtue were undermined long ago, and now, like Oswald, "worm-eaten" from within, are in danger of collapse.

Regine's lineage may also be doubtful. Her superb health, stressed throughout (she is "the picture of health" [151]), raises the question of whether she is Alving's daughter, or, if so, whether he actually had syphilis. Why else, one wonders, would Ibsen emphasize this in a play one of whose major motifs is inherited disease? It is possible is that Regine is in the third or "latent" stage of syphilis. If so, she will infect all who seek her out for her beauty. Ibsen's concern is the corruption hidden beneath the outwardly respectable and attractive surface, of which Regine would then provide an example. The Alving Home clearly affords another such example, and the Orphanage founded to paper over a multitude of sins still another.

Joanna's submission to the captain, and her association with the dissolute Engstrand before her employment by the Alvings, suggests a woman of easy virtue who might have had other lovers. Ibsen is careful to have Helene say only that the captain could not *deny* that Regine might be his child (129). He of course "couldn't deny it," given his "profligacy"; but he may not have been certain.

It is possible Joanna became pregnant by another, or did not know by whom she became pregnant. Realizing that Helene's suspicions would in any event result in termination of her employment, she might have claimed the captain as the father to obtain hush-money, and to secure a good place for her child in the future. Both were in fact the result. This woman "so precious genteel" (97), so proud of her association with "people who went to

Court" (98) would naturally prefer to believe that the father of her child was a Chamberlain.

If Regine cannot positively know who her father is, and if Oswald resembles her in this respect, then subplot mirrors main plot, and the Orphanage becomes the perfect symbol of that fundamental ambiguity and the behavior responsible.

The actual history of Helene's relationship to Manders or of Joanna's to possible lovers remains unknown. Ibsen deliberately gives us no assurances, only plausible alternatives. He wishes the very form of his drama to "model" the cosmos his protagonists inhabit; and in that cosmos, rife with concealment, possibilities necessarily replace truth.

The first act appropriately ends with an expression of the secretiveness, the furtiveness, the concealment of corruption that characterizes the whole. "Not a word—!" says Helene to Manders when they overhear Oswald accosting Regine in the dining-room (127).

Act II

Speaking of that incident, Manders observes that he is "completely unaccustomed to things of this kind"; and again "I am quite inexperienced in such matters" (128–129). But his fascination with Regine's charms and the subsequent conversation with Helene present a very different picture. Manders self-righteously declares, "Never—even in my secret thoughts—have I ever regarded you as anything but the wife of another." Had they been intimate emotionally or physically that would of course be false. And Helene implies it to be false: "Do you believe what you say? … One so easily forgets one's own feelings" (135). She certainly did not, in the past, try to conceal *her* feelings: "I thought you understood where what you call my heart had strayed to at that time," she says (130). It is clear from this that Helene revealed her love to Manders before her marriage. She nonetheless chose to wed Alving for his money and position, abandoning the man she truly loved and who obviously loved her. Resentment and envy as well as fear of scandal may have motivated Manders' subsequent rejection of her.

In any event, his remarks conflict with his declaration of detachment. He calls his rejection of Helene, "the hardest struggle of my life" and "greatest victory of my life" (134–35). This is hardly consistent with his insistence that he thought of her only as Alving's wife. Helene who then offered herself to him body and soul ("Here I am, take me!") objects that his rejection of her was "a wrong done to both of us." She clearly assumes, and Manders appears to confirm, they were then emotionally, if not physically, intimate. Her offer of herself implies at least that. If we accept her evaluation it is evident that the parson has simply "forgotten" that difficult past, and quite possibly other "details" such as physical intimacy. It is characteristic of him to avoid responsibility for disreputable actions. As noted, we see the beginning of a similar process at the close of the drama when Manders willingly permits Engstrand to assume blame for the fire. The parson will soon "forget" his possible complicity. We obviously cannot rely upon Manders for a truthful account of events that condemn him.

In this connection, consider his interaction in Act II with Engstrand. When he learns that Engstrand has for years deceived him and is not the father of Regine he says "from today everything is at an end between us." Engstrand, who fears the loss of support for his tavern-bordello responds: "Just suppose, sir, for a moment that your reverence was in the same predicament as my poor Joanna," meaning, obviously, "let us suppose Parson Manders that you, too, had an illegitimate child" (138). Manders of course vehemently denies the possibility. But Engstrand persists: "I mean suppose there were something your reverence were ashamed of in the eyes of the world, so to speak." Both remarks are barely veiled threats. The knowledge or rumor that prompts them may secretly inform Engstrand's earlier remark to Regine about the parson—"He's a chap to tell you what a child owes to his father" (101). Knowing that Joanna was in the Alvings' employ after Helene returned to the captain, Manders has reason to suspect that she may have overheard conversations between husband and wife implicating him, and passed that information on to Engstrand.

Manders can have no way of knowing what Engstrand knows and so succumbs to his insinuations, soon accepting Engstrand's obviously trumped up explanations as truth, forgiving his lies, indeed begging his pardon, and cementing their unholy alliance with a handshake. Although now aware that Engstrand is not Regine's father, and that Helene, for good reasons to which he assented only moments before, wants to protect the girl from him, Manders says shortly afterwards, "Engstrand must have help with his Sailors' Home. Regine must go home with him and give him her assistance" (155). How are we to explain this abrupt *volte-face* other than by the fact that he fears Engstrand may have something on him? When Helene later threatens to speak "openly" about the past in order to assuage Oswald's fears, Manders, not knowing where this might lead, frantically intervenes "But you won't do that! No, no, no!" (155). Does he fear for Oswald or for himself? Oswald has just said he plans to live with Regine—"as my wife—if she insists upon that."

Manders, who earlier condemned such "immoral" arrangements, can hardly be concerned about Oswald's morals.

Manders is not unique in this respect but exemplary. Helene gives two conflicting accounts of her life with her husband. And even when she proffers the "truth" she conceals from Oswald the fact that she once abandoned the captain for Manders. Oswald tells Helene that while abroad he "never lived recklessly in any sense," and so his affliction cannot be caused by profligacy (145). He portrays himself as an "innocent victim."[20] Yet, almost immediately after his return he attempts to seduce Regine—not even bothering to shut the door to the dining room—and begins drinking heavily. Is this what he means by "the joy of life"? Is his behavior the result of, or a reaction to, his affliction, and so atypical, or is it habitual? We cannot know. But it clearly casts doubt upon his assertion of innocence. He may indeed have been responsible for his illness.

This does not exclude the possibility of "inherited" disease. As noted, Oswald's alcoholism and lasciviousness are in Ibsen's view commonplace failings of fallen man, inherited from our first parents. Helene alludes briefly to this history when to justify a possible liaison between Oswald and Regine she refers to Genesis ("we are all descended from a union of that description, so we are told" [133]).

What, if anything, does Oswald overhear while enjoying his cigar alone in the dining room? Of Regine Helene says "Out of the house she shall go—and at once" (129). There is talk about Oswald and Regine marrying; about the captain's profligacy ("I ought to have said to Oswald, 'listen my son your father was a dissolute man'" [132]); about Helene's abandonment of the captain, her commitment to Manders and her cowardly attempts to conceal the truth; she admits to lying about the captain in her letters to Oswald. To be sure the door of the dining-room is closed. But Helene's "*stifled cry*" when she unexpectedly encounters Oswald there (143) suggests her desire to conceal the truth, her fear that the closed door may not have been sufficient, and her wish to hide from Oswald her desire for concealment.

Oswald clearly changes between acts one and two. Are we to attribute that to the progression of his disease, to his previous deliberate suppression of the truth, to new knowledge gained via a conversation overheard, or are all responsible? In the first act he remarks: "Oh, it's good to be at home again!" (115). When Manders says "A child's home is and always must be his proper place" Oswald replies "There I agree entirely with Mr. Manders." His alcoholism is then manifest only as frequent queries about when dinner will be ready—for then drinking is usual and permitted.

After he returns from the dining room he no longer attempts to conceal his craving for drink and his fears. He now says he is "afraid to stay at home." The "joy of life" would "degenerate into something ugly" there (154). "I cannot spend my life here," he says (151). Helene's remarks about her cowardly fear of disclosure might have something to do with this. Had he overheard her talk about dismissing Regine we would expect him to make known his own wishes concerning the girl, and he does. He says she embodies for him "the joy of life"; she offers "salvation" (152). He asks why Helene and Manders had been so quiet at dinner (150), and raises the issue of inherited disease (148). The last two points especially are suggestive. Oswald appears to suspect that the truth has been kept from him, as he might, had he overheard fragments of the conversation in the next room. "Mother, what is it that is being concealed from me?" he says (155).

The doctor's diagnosis, "The sins of the fathers are visited on the children," obviously makes a profound impression upon Helene; she twice repeats it. But what precisely she is thinking is obscure. It is clear that if the captain was syphilitic, Helene, who attended him and concealed his disease until his death, would have a very good idea of its consequences. Yet, when Oswald speaks of the "deadly fear" that possesses him she says "Fear? Fear of what? What do you mean?" (151). When he remarks that he despairs because his illness was his "own fault" and so as a result he has "disgracefully, stupidly, thoughtlessly thrown away [his] happiness, [his] health, everything in the world" she replies "No, no my darling boy; that is impossible … Things are not so desperate as you think" (148). She ignores the clear implication that his disease might be the consequence of his profligacy. Does she hope that the doctor was wrong? Is she simply reluctant to face the awful truth about her son? Does she believe that Oswald still may have many good years ahead of him before the disease takes its toll? Does she assume that since Oswald is not the captain's son he could not have inherited the disease from him? If she thinks Manders the father, her apparent shock upon learning of the possible role of "The sins of the father" is certainly understandable. How could the parson, that paragon of moral rectitude, be responsible for Oswald's affliction? Better to believe that the doctor was mistaken.

The Orphanage—*qua* refuge of unacknowledged, dispossessed children—is the very embodiment of hidden truths and silent sins. It exists to isolate them and cloak them in sanctity. Engstrand affords another example of corruption that masquerades as virtue. Just so, Manders' religiosity conceals his own sins—current, and past. Indeed, all protagonists are guilty of such deception. The conflagration that ends this act signifies the fatal consequences of concealment and subterfuge. The orphanage to be consecrated to God is in fact consecrated to the Adversary, whose element is fire, revealing its true nature as enabler of Engstrand, scion of the Father of Lies; for its destruction will fund his bordello. His "Sailors' Home" will bear the deceptive title of "Alving Home," concealing corruption beneath a veneer of respectability, just as the home of the Alvings did (161).

Act III

The stage direction reads, "*All the doors [to the various rooms] are standing open*" signaling the apparent end of attempts to suppress the truth in the Alving household. Furtive, secret conversations will be no more. But this "revolution" is an illusion. Manders and Engstrand, who enter almost immediately, agree in a softly spoken aside that Engstrand will take responsibility for the fire, which he accuses Manders of starting.

This accusation may also be false, another untruth in the maze of ambiguities and untruths that constitute *Ghosts*. In Act I Helene remarks upon Engstrand's carelessness with matches; he started a fire amidst some shavings in the Orphanage (111). In act II Manders asks Engstrand to light the Orphanage candles, another opportunity for carelessness (141). Manders disputes the manner in which Engstrand says he started the fire. But he would naturally say that to deflect suspicion even if guilty. Whatever the truth, it is certainly possible that Engstrand rather than Manders was responsible for the fire and falsely assumes responsibility in order to manipulate the parson, whose assistance he needs for his Sailors' Home. In an aside to Regine he says, "Now we've got the old fool, my girl" (158). Only the devilish Engstrand knows what actually happened. Fearful of even a breath of scandal, Manders does not contest his account, but readily succumbs to the blackmail.

Engstrand falsely represents his restaurant-bordello as a respectable refuge. Manders will finance and give his imprimatur to a lie—quite appropriate in view of his own evasiveness. He will facilitate a continuing cascade of untruths and transmitted disease. The "virtuous" parson's financial aid will enable Engstrand, a devil incarnate as it were, to disseminate without apparent limit the disease symbolic of original sin. Manders' contribution will enable the Alving Home to promote the corrupt behavior for which the parson condemns the home of the Alvings (156). And, because Manders has succumbed to Engstrand's blackmail, he will not in future be able to disengage unless the carpenter permits it, which is most unlikely.

Helene offers Oswald a new explanation of the captain's "profligate life," one which can be advanced "without destroying any one's ideals" (155). In this second version the captain is portrayed as the victim of confinement "in a second-rate town, which had none of the joy of life," but offered only the companionship of "idlers and tipplers," and of a wife for whom "Everything seemed to turn upon duty—my duty or his duty." "Your father," she says, "was [in consequence] a lost man [McFarlane, "a broken man"] before ever you were born" (164). One wonders whether this second, radically different version is truthful or dictated by Helene's desire to relieve Oswald of responsibility for his affliction. Would a dutiful woman have abandoned her husband after only a year of marriage? Of that incident Helene says nothing. She asks afterwards, "Now have I taken away all your remorse and self-reproach?" (168). The obvious implication is that Oswald's illness is inherited and not of his own doing as he had feared. She appears to be unaware or unconcerned that she may have just confirmed the existence of deadly inherited disease in her son. He clearly believes this as his sudden exclamation "*in a choking voice*" reveals (164). It is also surprising that notwithstanding her sympathetic reinterpretation of the captain's married life Helene evinces not the slightest interest in the utter destruction of his memorial, or in the disposition of his estate, which she leaves entirely in Manders' hands. Her indifference is precisely what it was in the first act, when she offered a very different explanation for Alving's profligacy. It is curious that Helene, who has just told Oswald that the captain was probably the source of his illness, and who deliberately prevented all communication or association with Alving during his lifetime, seems put out by her son's lack of filial affection. Is she perhaps distressed by Oswald's unwillingness to wholeheartedly accept what may be still another fictional account? Ewbank notes that her revised description of her life with the captain differs linguistically from the original. The former is characterized by "short, simple sentences" and "straightforward construction," as if she were impulsively revealing long suppressed truths. The latter is constructed of "a series of antithesis, as if she were thinking while speaking, as if the truth were being modified while uttered."[21] And that may be the case.

As noted, when Oswald speaks of his fear of a recurrent attack, Helene appears nonplussed: "The fear … I don't understand you. What fear do you mean—?" (168). Oswald complains that he is "not able to work." She responds: "You will soon find you are able to work again now, my dear boy. You have no longer all those painful depressing thoughts to brood over." She only responds with alarm when he remarks "What I am suffering from is hereditary;

it—(*touches his forehead, and speaks very quietly*)—it lies here." "*Almost speechless*" she says "Oswald! No-no!" "It isn't true, Oswald! It is impossible! It can't be that!" (169). And later, when Oswald exacts from her a promise to administer the morphia should it become necessary she responds "But it shan't become necessary. No, no—It is impossible it should!" She concludes, "It has only been a dreadful fancy of yours, Oswald. Nothing but a fancy. All this upset has been bad for you. But now you will get some rest, at home with your own mother, my darling boy … There, now. The attack is over. You see how easily it passed off! I knew it would …" (172).

It is difficult to justify her responses if her husband was in fact syphilitic, and if she believes the disease was transmitted by him to her child, or even suspects this might have been the case. As we have several times noted, she cared for the captain during his illness and would have been thoroughly familiar with the progress of the disease. Helene is aware of the doctor's diagnosis and of his observation that "The sins of the fathers are visited on the children," which can only mean inherited disease such as syphilis. To relieve Oswald of his "remorse and self reproach" she has just implied that his illness was not his own fault but inherited from his father, "a lost [or "broken"] man" before he was born. The logical, inevitable conclusion is that Oswald has in all probability inherited mind-destroying syphilis. Either Helene cannot accept this truth *which she has herself just conveyed*—an incongruous and inexplicable reaction—or she believes that Alving was not syphilitic but afflicted with some other terminal disease of profligacy such as cirrhosis, or if syphilitic that Manders, not Alving, was the father and that therefore Oswald could not have inherited his affliction from that source, and so his fears are groundless. She cannot reveal this last option to her son without exposing her past infidelity and compromising the parson. All indications are that until she hears that the disease has attacked the brain she regards it as something much less threatening. And when Oswald tells her it resides there, she refuses to accept it, thinking it "impossible."

Some are troubled by Helene's apparent acceptance of an incestuous union between Oswald and Regine. Brian Downs, to the contrary, thinks "The calm manner in which Mrs. Alving … contemplated the possibility, even the desirability, of an incestuous union between Oswald and Regine … [indicative of] the distance by which Ibsen had outstripped most of his co-evals in the acceptance of the new science."[22] There is another, simpler, explanation for Helene's unusual behavior: she believes, or prefers to believe, that Oswald was not the captain's child but Manders', and that he and Regine are, therefore, not half-brother and sister.

We can as little know the truth in this case as in the others. Neither Helene nor Oswald can be certain of how he acquired "the French disease," which after all might have been the consequence of his Parisian stay, transmitted by Alving, or inherited from Manders. Helene's terminal, horrified reaction reflects not simply indecisiveness, but all-encompassing ignorance, which as we have seen Ibsen associates with blindness and darkness. For reasons which she cannot know Helene faces the prospect of nursing a syphilitic—a ghost—or administering the fatal morphia. That, too, remains undecided, and so unknown by her as well as by the audience. The blind Oswald's "sun," emblematic of truth, is, and will forever remain, invisible and unattainable in this cosmos. Francis Fergusson and others who regard the ending of *Ghosts* as "unsatisfactory" are clearly mistaken.[23] Ibsen's incomplete ending perfectly completes and concentrates in one intense moment the significance of this enigmatic tale of concealed motives, obscure responsibilities, and alternative realities.

Notes

1. Eric Bentley, "In Search of Theater" in McFarlane, *Henrik Ibsen: A Critical Anthology*, 262.
2. Max Nordau, *Degeneration*, 368.
3. Hermann J. Weigand, *Modern Ibsen*, 91.
4. Hugh Kenner, "Joyce and Ibsen's Naturalism" in Lyons, *Critical Essays*, 65–66.
5. Alexis Soloski, "The Great Imitator," 290.
6. Alexis Soloski, "The Great Imitator," 289.
7. Joan Templeton, "Of This Time," 58, 59.
8. Russell Brown, "Taking Ghosts," 92.
9. F. W. Kaufmann, "Ibsen's Conception of Truth" in Fjelde, *Ibsen: A Collection*, 25.
10. John Northam, *Critical Study*, 84.
11. James Joyce "Epilogue to Ibsen's 'Ghosts'" in McFarlane, *Henrik Ibsen: A Critical Anthology*, 383–385.
12. Daniel Haakonsen, "Ibsen's realisme," in McFarlane, *Henrik Ibsen: A Critical Anthology*, 290.
13. Daniel Haakonsen cited by Brian Crow in "Romantic Ambivalence," 208.
14. Evert Sprinchorn argues that Ibsen was familiar with the writing of the nineteenth-century syphilologist, Alfred Fournier (Soloski, "The Great Imitator," 293). And "Fournier describes several case studies in which syphilis is transmitted via casual household contact, such as a kiss" (Soloski, "The Great Imitator,"300).
15. Inge-Stina Ewbank translation, from "Ibsen's Dramatic Language as a Link between his 'Realism' and his 'Symbolism'," in Lyons, *Critical Essays*, 71.
16. Inge-Stina Ewbank in Lyons, *Critical Essays*, 71.
17. Hermann J. Weigand, *Modern Ibsen*, 82.

18. Charles Leland, "In Defense," 409–411.
19. A. F. Machiraju, "Ideals and Victims," 138.
20. Hermann J. Weigand concurs; v. *Modern Ibsen*, 93.
21. Inge-Stina Ewbank in Lyons, *Critical Essays*, 71.
22. Brian Downs in Lyons, *Critical Essays*, 124.
23. Francis Fergusson in Fjelde, *Critical Essays*, 116.

References

All parenthetical page citations in this text are from *Eleven Plays of Henrik Ibsen*, ed. B. A. Cerf, D. S. Klopfer. New York: *The Modern Library*, 1935. Translators not given but those of plays discussed in this volume appear to be R. Farquharson Sharp (*Ghosts*, *An Enemy of the People*), Edmund Gosse and William Archer (*The Master Builder*, *Hedda Gabler*), and William Archer (*The Wild Duck*). I found those older translations satisfactory for my purposes. In the few cases where translation appeared to be an issue I have appended parallel citations from *The Oxford Ibsen* (McFarlane, James Walter, ed. and trans. *The Oxford Ibsen*, 8 vols. London: Oxford University Press, 1962).

Brown, Russell. "Taking Ghosts to the Doctor." *Tijdschrift Voor Skandinavistiek* 13, no.1 (1992): 91–103.

Crow, Brian. "Romantic Ambivalence in 'The Master Builder.'" *Studies in Romanticism* 20, no. 2 (Summer 1981): 202–223.

Fjelde, Rolf, ed. *Ibsen: A Collection of Critical Essays*. Englewood Cliffs, NJ: Prentice-Hall, 1965.

Kenner, Hugh. "Joyce and Ibsen's Naturalism." in Lyons, Charles R., ed. *Critical Essays on Henrik Ibsen*. Boston: G. K. Hall & Co., 1987.

Leland, Charles. "In Defense of Pastor Manders." *Modern Drama* 21, no. 4 (Winter 1978): 405–420.

Lyons, Charles R., ed. *Critical Essays on Henrik Ibsen*. Boston: G. K. Hall & Co., 1987.

Machiraju, A. F. "Ideals and Victims: Ibsen's Concerns in *Ghosts* and *The Wild Duck*." *Modern Language Review* 87, no. 1 (January 1992): 134–142.

McFarlane, James, ed. *Henrik Ibsen: A Critical Anthology*. Harmondsworth, Middlesex, England: Penguin Books, 1970.

Nordau, Max. *Degeneration*. New York: Appleton, 1912.

Northam, John. *Ibsen: A Critical Study*. Cambridge: Cambridge Universty Press, 1973.

Soloski, Alexis. "'The Great Imitator': Staging Syphilis in a Doll House and Ghosts." *Modern Drama* 56, no. 3 (Fall 2013): 287–305.

Templeton, Joan. "Of This Time, of This Place: Mrs. Alving's Ghosts and the Shape of the Tragedy." *PMLA* 101, no. 1 (January 1986): 57–68.

Weigand, Hermann J. *The Modern Ibsen*. New York: Henry Holt & Co., 1925.

· 2 ·

WHO IS IBSEN'S ENEMY OF THE PEOPLE?

Prefatory

As noted in the *Introduction* misinterpretations of *An Enemy of the People* stem chiefly from the persistent tendency to regard Doctor Thomas Stockmann as a "mouthpiece" for Ibsen. Weigand's critique is typical. The play was a response to the "abusive criticism" of *Ghosts*. "[H]e would not have been Ibsen, had he not boiled inwardly with rage over the stupidity and hypocritical cant of his detractors. But fortunately rage subsided into derisive humor; and in that frame of mind he conceived and wrote his ringing dramatic defense, 'An Enemy of the People,' … for the Doctor's ideas about society, as well as the vehement and paradoxical form of their utterance are Ibsen's own."[1] Edmund Gosse asserts that "The hero … is a sort of Henrik Ibsen in practical life … and the play is really a piece of rather violent personal polemic."[2] Robert Brustein, reflecting the traditional view, thinks Stockmann the only "idealist" Ibsen does not condemn.[3] Thomas Van Lann notes that "whether warranted or not, this standard view continues to gain adherents; as recently as 1980, Bernard F. Dukore concluded his analysis of the play by coming down four-square as a staunch advocate of the prevailing view: "Clearly, Dr. Stockmann's interpretation of events is Ibsen's."[4] The play has been criticized on this account. For

Eric Bentley "*An Enemy of the People* is inferior Ibsen just because it is one of the few plays in which this author seems simply to be 'telling us'—with upraised finger and an inclination to be very angry if we aren't good and do as we're 'told.'"[5]

Stockmann's obvious flaws posed difficulties for adherents of the traditional view and they "developed various strategies for accommodating them," none of which were entirely satisfactory. Of late there has been a reassessment. Van Laan observes that "Recognition of Dr. Stockmann's 'temperamental and very human weaknesses' has increased over the years, and recently it has prompted some commentators to take those weaknesses not as details to be accommodated but as sources of departure for new readings that break sharply from the standard view."[6] Unfortunately, Van Laan's reassessment is vitiated by his belief that "it is essentially irrelevant to the problem with which the play deals that Dr. Stockmann's chief adversary should be his brother."[7] Richard Hornby's reassessment is of more interest. For him "*An Enemy of the People* ... is not a presentation of truth, with a protagonist who serves as the dramatist's spokesman, but rather a study of how people—including the protagonist—respond to a truth in the light of their own human limitations and needs and bend it, consciously or otherwise, to their own purposes."[8]

In fact, the subject matter of *An Enemy of the People* is not as commonly assumed "one brave man's struggle to do the right thing and speak the truth in the face of extreme social intolerance." Neither is it about the conflict of the abstract concepts "Makten" ("Might") and "Retten" ("Right") as Ewbank maintains;[9] nor is it only about the irreconcilable conflict of two brothers—although that is nearer the truth. Ibsen's chief concern is the same "life-lie" central to his next play, *The Wild Duck*, written two years later. In *An Enemy of the People* it takes the form of the lies one tells oneself and others—manifest as the firm belief in the integrity and purity of one's motives—to justify what is in fact self-aggrandizing egotism. This is as characteristic of Dr. Thomas Stockmann, ostensibly the "hero" of Ibsen's drama, as it is of the other personae. Stockmann's defense of the truth permits his escape from the truth; his revelations of others' weaknesses conceal his own. Ibsen confronts him with a series of temptations and to each he succumbs, becoming progressively more egocentric and isolated. His evolution ends inevitably in the egotistical conclusion that "the strongest man in the world is he who stands most alone" (288).

If Stockmann's flaws are not immediately apparent, that is because, as Haakonsen contends, Ibsen has here, as in the other dramas we consider, "established a literary form which created one impression in the theatre and another, completely opposite, impression from careful reading and study of the texts. When a normal audience has seen one of Ibsen's plays performed on the stage, it will retain an impression of having seen characters with an idealistic bent. But the scholar who … can see various parts of the dialogue in context realizes that this impression is but an illusion. What the author presents to the attentive reader is, in fact, a caricature of idealism, an exposure of the kind of idealism which holds theatre audiences."[10]

The early history of the protagonists is crucial. As in *Ghosts* the sins of the parent are transmitted to the child, with the proviso that by "sins" Ibsen refers not to the beliefs of a specific religion, but rather to failings that afflict all of mankind, and so are coincident with birth.

Thomas Stockmann insists that he and his brother Peter are "descended from some old rascal of a pirate from Pomerania or thereabouts" (260). And the piratical disposition *is* characteristic of both. They would both control the (unnamed) town's affairs and so take possession of it, as the pirate does of the vessels he boards. Their conflict centers about who shall rule. This impulse is obvious in the case of the overbearing, egocentric Peter. In Thomas it is obscured by superficial altruism but is no less active. The two are, after all, brothers. In Peter's case it is clear that pride and ambition masquerade as concern for the common welfare. A careful reading of the play reveals that this equally true of Thomas.

Their names are significant. Thomas, scientist and atheist, recalls the biblical "doubting Thomas." Peter, who assumes that he has the right to dictate both the moral and material behavior of the town where he is mayor, is named for Simon Peter, the Rock, from whom the Pope derives his dictatorial authority. The uncompromising, absolutist Petra (feminine of Peter) exhibits the same authoritarian tendencies.

Thomas's son Morton has inherited the piratical disposition of his father. He imagines growing up to be a pagan, "who shall be allowed to do anything [I] like" (191) and a Viking who pillages (190). He is aptly named after Morton Kiil. Indifferent to the consequences for the town, Kiil has polluted and exploited the land for profit. Thomas's daughter Petra is a "freethinker" who does not believe in a "supernatural power" that rewards the virtuous and punishes the vicious (she condemns the English story she is asked to translate on that account; [229]), or, presumably, in sin, which might serve as a check on the piratical instincts. (It will become clear that Ibsen critiques her philosophy. For while a beneficent God is absent from this exposé of the "life-lie," the Father of Lies, the Devil, is indisputably active.)

The recent history of the brothers is also relevant. Ibsen consigns Thomas to penury, isolation, and virtual impotence in the frigid north among the poorest of the poor, and stations his relatively affluent brother in the warmer south in a position of authority to establish conditions for envy and a basis for Thomas's subsequent attempts to appropriate his brother's office and prestige. It makes this man, so long neglected by others, particularly vulnerable to the praise that progressively inflates his ego. Ibsen does not give a reason for Thomas's exile because he does not need to. We perceive at the end, when Thomas once more "stands alone," the personal characteristics that inevitably led to it.

Mrs. Stockmann accuses her husband of antagonizing Peter "again," (186). The implication is that Thomas in the past clashed repeatedly with his brother. Peter's critique of what he characterizes as Thomas's obstinacy and disregard for authority (213–214) refers to that history and, in effect, confirms it. His condemnation of Thomas in the first act (185–186)—whom he accuses of going behind the backs of those in charge of the Baths (see below)—and Thomas' strong reaction establish that mutual hostility still qualifies their relationship. Its persistence suggests that the two will remain at loggerheads indefinitely; and the drama bears this out. Their radically different natures (save for the ambition to rule)—which may have been suggested to Ibsen by the traditional contrast between the contemplative and active life—supplies a basis for their antipathy. Thomas is intellectual; Peter is practical; Thomas is generous; Peter is close-fisted; Thomas is a gregarious family man; Peter has no family; Thomas is innovative and politically liberal; Peter is cautious and politically conservative; Thomas is a *bon vivant*; Peter subsists on tea and toast.

During his years of exile Thomas submits frequent essays dealing with civil matters to the "*People's Messenger*," the local paper in his former town, (213–214). Chief among them is a proposal that the town establish a spa to bring visitors and business. Thomas prefers to regard such suggestions as evidence of his compassionate interest in the general welfare. Subsequent events suggest something quite different: namely, that those attempts to influence the town's affairs are early instances of his desire to curry favor with its citizenry preparatory to challenging, with the intent of replacing, his brother, the town's mayor and de-facto ruler. He is the unnamed "authority" whom Thomas repeatedly challenges via the *Messenger*.

After years of apparently fruitless broadsides (214, 253) Thomas's proposal for the Baths is accepted. But its implementation is faulty. Thomas questions the arrangement of the piping bringing water to the Baths. He writes the *Messenger*, protesting that this oversight could in future create difficulties; but his protests are ignored (195). To prevent possible future criticism of the project and of himself Peter ends his brother's exile so that he can control and contain him (213). He offers Thomas the subordinate position of attending physician of the Baths. This stratagem recoils, in fact affording the irrepressible, combative Thomas new opportunities to condemn his brother. He subsequently attributes the faulty execution of his plan, and the ensuing deadly pollution of the Baths, to the negligence or stupidity of Peter, "Chairman of the governing body of the Baths" (185). "It was owing to your action," he says, "that both the Baths and the water-conduits were built where they are; and that is what you won't acknowledge—that damnable blunder of yours" (211–212).

His new role significantly improves Thomas's financial prospects. However, it offends him that his rival and antagonist is his superior (just as it doubtless pleases Peter). In conformity with long-standing ambition he hopes to invert the relationship. Any such ambition is of course inconsistent with his self-image as a disinterested scientist who has only the welfare of the public in mind. It resides in his unconscious, or what in Ibsen passes for the unconscious. But that triumph over Peter, not the well being of society, is his ultimate goal becomes perfectly clear with the unfolding of events.

Illness among the Bath's patrons during the previous season leads Thomas to suspect that the Baths may be polluted and a danger to public health (193). He attempts to determine the cause and sends off a sample of the waters for analysis. This investigation occupies him "the whole winter." "I have been quietly working the whole winter for the welfare of the town," he says (237). The timing of his submission is significant. An election is in the offing which will determine Peter's future (188). If Thomas is to discredit his brother preparatory to usurping his authority, he must do so before that event, which otherwise will almost certainly return Peter to office. Thomas is anxious to receive the test results beforehand, and repeatedly asks after the mail that will bring them (183, 186, 189).

There are other reasons for his anxiety. It is only owing to his association with the Baths, which were originally his idea, that Thomas enjoys whatever reputation he has among the townspeople. Hovstad, editor-in-chief of the *Messenger*, reflects the common view when he asserts that the Baths "owe their existence to him" (180). If there should be pollution, and if faulty piping should *not* prove to be its cause, the whole project will perhaps become suspect and possibly irredeemable, for which Thomas will be blamed. Should the baths prove to be polluted because of mislaid piping, Thomas will be vindicated and Peter condemned. If nothing is wrong with the Baths things will remain as they are and Thomas's hopes of replacing Peter will vanish. Although that outcome would be the most favorable for the town and for the Bath's patrons, it is not the one this "benevolent," "idealistic" man of science desires.

Before he receives the analysis of the waters Thomas writes an article for publication by the *Messenger* which assumes that the Baths *are* polluted and that mislaid piping *is* the cause (195). Although he certainly would not admit it to himself or to others, those are the analytical results he hopes for; hence his premature, critical article. And his hopes reveal his agenda. Composed shortly prior to the action depicted onstage (195), ready to publish before the immanent election, the article, "four closely written sheets," is not merely a warning to the owners of the Baths—which should have been sufficient given Thomas's official responsibilities—but a violent attack, leveled against the authorities responsible for the faulty implementation of his proposal and so for the pollution (221). Chief among them is Peter, who led the project.

Act I

In order to replace Peter Thomas must have the support of the *Messenger*. Therefore it is not surprising that he invites the financially strapped editor and his assistant to regularly dine at his table upon food they could not otherwise afford, and which for that matter Thomas himself cannot afford given that his expenses exceed his income (184). (Hovstad and Billing have their own hidden motives for visiting Thomas and encouraging his ambitions other than the prospect of a good meal. They are rivals for the hand of Thomas's daughter Petra, who they expect will inherit a substantial fortune from the tanner Kiil, adoptive father of her mother.)

That display of munificence reflects Thomas's egotistical indifference to the needs of family members when they conflict with his own. (One is reminded of Hjalmar Ekdal in *The Wild Duck*.) It anticipates his decision in the final act to impoverish them utterly rather than sacrifice his inflated conception of self. It also figures as an early "salvo" in the constant warfare between the brothers. Thomas tempts Peter, who is visiting, with delectable meat that he may desire but, as Thomas knows, cannot accept because of his "wretched digestion" (183, 186). He draws attention to the relative opulence that his conservative brother will find objectionable, and to the familial camaraderie from which the lonely Peter who "has no home comforts of any kind" (187) is excluded.

When Thomas first enters he deliberately ignores his brother (182). His subsequent observation that he finds it "very delightful" to see Peter cannot be true, especially in view of the article, already written, that condemns those responsible for the misrouting of the bath conduits, an error which, as noted, Thomas attributes to Peter. Thomas begins their conversation with praise of the young people brimming with new ideas who will supplant "old fogies" like Peter and himself, an observation bound to offend the conservative, authoritarian Peter. And Peter predictably does take offense (182–183).

Thomas interrupts their conversation to ask his wife if the postman has arrived (183). His thoughts turn to this because of the preceding acrimonious dispute with his brother. He anxiously and nervously awaits the results of the specimen submitted for analysis (189), which could ruin him, implicate Peter, or preserve the status quo favorable to Peter.

Thomas's reaction when he learns that the water supply and Baths are contaminated with deadly pathogens because of mislaid piping is not at all what one would expect from a benevolent, public-spirited man of science. He is hugely pleased, having hoped for precisely that determination. As Richard Hornby notes, "he is *happy* that the baths are polluted."[11] There is pollution for which Peter, not he, is responsible. His "great discovery" will establish his reputation as a scientist. It will refute those who, "as usual" thought his ideas the figments of "a crazy man's imagination" (192, 195). He means not only the tanner Kiil, who has criticized him in the past, but especially his brother, whose attitude in that regard Thomas is well aware of and Ibsen soon establishes (213–214). "If only I had Peter here now!" he says (192). Thomas habitually rubs his hands together when he is especially pleased (208, 270), and does so when he observes immediately afterward that "All the conduit-pipes will have to be relaid" (195). Peter was responsible for that fatal error and the pollution arises from Krill's tannery and so both of his critics will be undone. (Michael Meyer suggests that the disease caused by the pollution was probably cholera.[12] As in *Ghosts*, to name it would be to obscure its metaphorical meaning. Ibsen, who is concerned with moral as well as physical pollution, deliberately does not.)

When Billing observes that in consequence of his "discovery" Thomas is "going to be the foremost man in town" Thomas reacts "happily" (196). He professes disinterest, rejecting a possible "testimonial" and "increase in salary." But his very protestations reveal his expectations. As Peter correctly observes, Thomas habitually thinks his contributions overlooked ("you insist that you have been neglected and persecuted" [213]), not an unusual complaint for an egotist such as he. His "discovery" will perhaps rectify that, and may even permit him to replace Peter as the leading citizen. Hence his *public* revelation of the danger, which can only increase his status and diminish Peter's.

Although Thomas's report is addressed to members of the governing board of the Baths who have substantial investments in the project and, one would think, should be given an opportunity to respond to the findings before they are made public, Thomas at once announces them to assembled friends and family (192–194), directs Petra to notify Kiil (195), and agrees that Hovstad can immediately print a summary in the "*Messenger*" (195). Peter, chair of the board, is to receive notice of his brother's findings not before these irrevocable steps are taken, as he had requested (185) and as reason and prudence would seem to dictate, but at the same time. Hovstad, who, as Thomas knows, has his own axe to grind with the governing elite, asserts that "It is very desirable that the public should be informed of [the pollution] without delay," by which he means the very next day (206). And Thomas concurs. He prefers to believe the fiction that his sole motive is to serve his native town and its citizens (196), rather than concede that envy and ambition drive him. But fiction it is. And so it is understandable that when circumstances change and those he was "happy" to serve reject him, this professed public spirited scientist rejects them, and says no more of the need to purify the Baths for the sake of the common good. To the contrary, he sees in the pollution an opportunity to ruin the town that has shunned him.

Act II

Mrs. Stockmann (197), Kiil (199), and Hovstad (202) are of course aware of Peter's responsibility for the implementation of the Bath project. They know that he will not take kindly to Thomas's accusation of incompetence shortly before the election, and they point this out directly or indirectly to Thomas. Thomas has written a "crushing" critique of the misbegotten enterprise in which "Every word falls like … the blow of a sledgehammer" upon the individuals responsible (221). Peter has told him that all communications concerning such issues must proceed "through the proper channels," meaning Peter himself (185). And although Thomas immediately sends Peter a copy of his findings (195), he does not consult him before publicly announcing them and giving Hovstad permission to print a summary at the earliest opportunity.

Indeed, by revealing his findings to Kill, Petra, Hovstad, Billing and Aslaksen Thomas has insured that they will soon become common knowledge, with or without publication of his "crushing" criticism. He justifies his premature, precipitous revelation to himself and to others by insisting that Peter will "be very glad that such an important truth has been brought to light" (195)—"Oh, he really will be pleased enough you know" (197); "It seems to me that the thing should go of itself" (206); "You will see that everything will run quite smoothly, Mr. Hovstad, quite smoothly" (207)—and deflects or minimizes other possible objections by Peter. In part this is owing to burgeoning egotism that can neither conceive nor brook any objections, in part to Thomas's need to believe his efforts motivated by scientific objectivity and altruism. To admit that he knew or suspected beforehand that Peter would object to his "discovery" and his "crushing" article would be to concede that the defeat of Peter, not the well-being of the populace, was always his primary goal. And that is a truth he cannot acknowledge. Encouraged by, and succumbing to, the praise of others, he has positioned himself as, and believes himself to be, the "savior" of the town.

Kiil remarks, "You keep up this game for all its worth; you won't repent it. I'm damned if you will!" (200). (McFarlane: "I'm damned sure you won't lose by it.") He is one of several "tempters" announced or accompanied by Ibsen's many references to the Devil and Underworld. He is followed immediately by Hovstad, who puts his paper at Thomas's disposal (208) and points out to him the larger implications of his crusade. Moral pollution is the real issue, he says. The enemy is "The morass that the whole life of our town is built on and is rotting in" (201). Thomas apparently had not thought of this. "What the deuce are you driving at," he says. (McFarlane: "What kind of damned nonsense is this you're talking, Mr. Hovstad?") Hovstad, too, is a tempter, and his words further amplify Thomas's sense of self-importance. Hovstad, he later says, has convinced him that his "discovery has a much wider bearing that [he] at first imagined" (208).

(In an early review Arne Garborg complains "there is a great deal of violent swearing" in *Enemy of the People*. Stockmann has been called "the most profane character in all of Ibsen."[13] None of this profanity is accidental, or inserted simply for the sake of "realism." Rather, it is Ibsen's way of denoting ubiquitous evil, especially when manifest as self-serving, self-deceiving lies. For the Devil is the very Father of Lies. The common epithet "by God's death" leaves the field to him altogether.)

The next "tempter" to appear is Aslaksen, who offers the support of the "compact majority." "[D]evil take it!" Thomas says when he hears Aslaksen's knock (203). (McFarlane: "damn it.") Aslaksen proposes "some kind of address of thanks from the townsmen for [Thomas's] share in a matter of such importance to the community" (205). And the prospect of notoriety, previously rejected by Thomas ("No my good friends, don't let us have any of that nonsense. I won't hear of anything of the kind" [196]), is now gladly accepted by him: "I can't tell you, dear Mr. Aslaksen, how extremely pleased I am to find such hearty support among my fellow citizens. I am delighted—delighted" (205). Thomas again succumbs to temptation, sinking ever deeper into the moral "morass" of self-regard.

Only after the visits of the "tempters" does Thomas insist that he talk with Peter before publication of Hovstad's summary of his findings (207). He feels that he can now safely do so, having been convinced by the apparent support of Kiil, Hovstad and Aslaksen that even should his brother object it will not deflect the avalanche that must soon crush him. Any negotiations with Peter will now be made from a position of strength. Thomas will at last be able to demonstrate his superiority, put his brother in his place. He agrees with Hovstad that if the "Mayor refuses to take the matter up" his damning article should be printed in its entirety (207).

The arrogance encouraged by others (208) prepares Thomas for his uncompromising confrontation with Peter. What appears to be a disagreement about what must be done to remedy the pollution of the Baths is in fact a ruthless contest of wills motivated by self interest. The brothers are not fully conscious of this. Both prefer to believe the "life-lie" that they selflessly promote the common good.

Although Peter does not assert this openly, it is clear that he suspects Thomas's motives. He questions his brother's assertion that the Baths are polluted, believing that Thomas exaggerates the actual extent of contamination for reasons of his own. He points out that it would be prohibitively expensive and time-consuming to reroute the pipes as Thomas recommends. It would mean the end of the Baths and of the income that has transformed the town. He argues that "for the common good," and for the sake of his reputation, which provides the "moral authority" that enables him to implement the common good (as he conceives it), Thomas's "report should not be delivered to the [Baths] Committee. In the interests of the public, you must withhold it" he says. If a revision of the piping is required, he, not Thomas, must take credit for it: "I will raise the question" he says (212). Peter argues that he acts on behalf of the town; for, as noted, that is the "life-lie" which this conceited, officious bureaucrat prefers to believe. His real concern is not the common good, but rather the damage the revelation of his incompetence will do to his standing in the community. It could very well end his mayoral career. Thomas might "reign" in his stead. For, as Thomas reminds him, the pollution is entirely Peter's fault, and that must become evident. Peter oversaw the project, and advertised his role (180–181). "It was owing to your action," Thomas says, "that both the Baths and the water conduits were built where they are; and that is what you won't acknowledge—that damnable blunder of yours" (211–212).

Peter's motives may be suspect, but his critique of Thomas's "solution" is not. Thomas would destroy the very baths he would save. If word of the pollution got abroad it would permanently cripple the economy of the town. Had Thomas really put the interests of the community first he almost certainly would have followed a different course. He would not publicly have revealed the pollution before taking his concerns to the Baths Committee and discussing with them possible remedies. As his subsequent conversation with Peter reveals (210), he was at the time unaware of the practical impossibility of implementing his "solution" and relaying the pipes. The season was not yet upon them and for all Thomas then knew it might have been possible to remedy the defects before its inception. Surely he realized that publication of the danger before consulting the Baths Committee would antagonize its members and his brother, its chief, who would have to implement any solution, and jeopardize the future of the town.

His impetuous, counterproductive behavior is not the result of his "artless" nature as Weigand asserts;[14] nor is he "simple-minded" as McFarlane assumes.[15] Thomas's real if unacknowledged and unconscious purpose was never to save the Baths and so serve the common good. He wished to implicate, to condemn, and to supplant his brother. And that required him to publicize the dangerous pollution and the need for a complete revision of the faulty piping for which his brother was responsible. His premature revelation of the cause of the pollution can be traced to the "wonderful" opportunity afforded by the technical analysis. Finally, he "had" Peter. He insists upon disclosure even when subsequently shown its disastrous consequences for his beloved town. Revision of the piping would be extremely costly and would require shutting down the baths for two years—permanently ending the monopoly and income of the town. His real motivation becomes clear with his subsequent disastrous defeat by Thomas before the assembled townspeople. This worst of all offenders condemns them, and indeed all of mankind, who put self-interest before the truth. The need to prevent infection of the Baths' patrons is forgotten, or remembered only in the context of the harm adverse publicity might do to those whom he now hates.

With respect to the arguments advanced by the brothers, Peter is obviously correct about the consequences to the town should the Baths be closed, and Thomas correct about the consequences to public health should they remain open. But their apparent and actual motives are very different. Peter would minimize the dangers ostensibly for the sake of the common good, but in fact to protect his reputation. Thomas would emphasize the dangers ostensibly for the sake of the common good but in fact to destroy Peter's reputation and magnify his own. Clearly, neither the common good, nor respect for the truth is really the issue. And as the brother's conversation becomes progressively more heated both fade from view. They are supplanted by personal invective revealing the enmity always latent beneath the politic surface. Thomas accuses Peter of blundering mismanagement which he would conceal through criminal lies (211); Peter accuses Thomas of having a "restless, pugnacious, rebellious disposition" (213), of cantankerous impetuosity, of ever complaining of the authorities and government (213).

Before Peter learns that Thomas has already publicized his findings, he proposes to do whatever he can to rectify the pollution, but unobtrusively: "[W]e will do our best privately; but nothing of this unfortunate affair—not a single word of it—must come to the ears of the public" (212). When he learns that the word is already out, he perceives that Thomas means to use the mismanagement of the project to attack and condemn him at a critical juncture in his career. Only then does he become as "crushing" as Thomas in his written critique. He warns Thomas that this could again impoverish him and his family, functioning in that respect as still another "tempter." "What the deuce [McFarlane: 'What the devil'] do you mean?" says Thomas. (212). He insists that Thomas, in his official capacity, surrender all independence, submit to his authority and renounce his "discovery."

As noted at the outset of this study the "piratical" brothers long contested for dominance. And it is Peter's assertion of his right to rule Thomas absolutely rather than Thomas's commitment to the common good or to the truth that induces Thomas to fight on, whatever the consequences for himself, for his family, or for his town and its fellow citizens. He now knows that if he persists in his course of action the baths will become known as a plague spot, ending the town's new found prominence and wealth. But that does not dissuade him. The defeat of his brother and egotistic self-regard have taken precedence over all else. He will not "bow" to Peter even to preserve the future of his children (220). Animalistic, atavistic instincts begin to predominate in this exponent of higher values: "I ought to have … shown my teeth!—bitten," he says (213). One is also reminded of the demons that torment the damned in early religious art. And indeed Thomas descends into an Underworld reserved for those who think only of self. For his part, Peter, who now clearly perceives that Thomas is out to ruin him, resolves to take any actions necessary to stop him, whatever the consequences for the unwitting patrons of the Baths. The animosity of the combatants becomes more prominent and their behavior more extreme to the degree that each feels his sense of self-importance and self-respect threatened.

Act III

Ibsen's peripheral characters—Hovstad, Billing, Aslaksen, Kiil, and Petra—all in their own way succumb to the life-lie. Material self-interest induces the first three "idealistic" exponents of social progress to abandon their leader, Thomas. But that is not the reason that they give for their change of heart, or the one in which they prefer to believe. It is rather that Thomas has "represented [his] case in a false light" (241). They are not at fault, he is. The "poisonous" pollution of the Baths is no longer an issue—indeed is denied, although the protagonists, having read Thomas's article, know this to be false. Kiil refuses to accept the truth that he is responsible for the pollution. He would be remembered as the philanthropist he clearly is not, and manipulates his fortune to insure this (278–279). Petra has abandoned belief in a benevolent God only to replace it with uncritical, misguided worship of Thomas, he of the "big generous heart" (231), who, in her eyes, can do no wrong.

Her role is that of "facilitator." Shaped by Thomas to be the worshipful devotee this egotist must have, she blindly accepts his accounts of what is true and what is false, what is noble and what ignoble, thereby supporting and enabling his "life-lie." We find her likeness in the "facilitators" of the *The Wild Duck*, (Gina Ekdal, Hedvig and Relling), of *The Master Builder* (Hilde Wangle), and of *John Gabriel Borkman* (Vilhelm Foldal). Within the cosmos defined by those dramas and in *An Enemy of the People* all succumb to the life-lie. Even the practical, clear-sighted Mrs. Stockmann at length becomes a victim.

Buoyed by what he believes to be the certain support of the *Messenger* and the "compact majority," motivated by envy and hatred of his brother—emotions now only too apparent—egotistically intent upon winning at all costs, Thomas tells the *Messenger* to print his "crushing" critique precisely as written, omitting not an "exclamation." Unwilling to acknowledge that lower rather than higher instincts drive him, he refers his hostility not to Peter, its actual source and target, but to an ambiguous and indefinite "they" who have nothing to do with the case:

> [T]hey have tried to rob me of my most elementary rights as a man— … they have tried to degrade me, to make a coward of me, to force me to put personal interests before my most sacred convictions … Well, they will get the worst of it with me … every single day I will bombard them with one article after another like bombshells— … I shall smite them to the ground—I shall crush them—I shall break down all their defenses before the eyes of the honest public! That is what I shall do! (224)

The nearly biblical language of this diatribe anticipates Thomas's subsequent egotistical elevation of self through identification with two beleaguered religious leaders, Luther and Christ.

Thomas's desire to supplant his brother as leader of the community, always a primary driving force, now rises from the depths to the surface of the drama. In a gesture at once comic and tragic he usurps the tokens of mayoral authority that Peter has left behind in the *Messenger*'s office—his hat and stick—and when Peter reenters confronts him as the "Mayor" who has replaced him:

Peter Stockmann.	What does this tomfoolery mean?
Dr. Stockmann.	Be respectful my good Peter. I am the chief authority in the town now.
Mrs. Stockmann (almost in tears).	Really, Thomas!
Peter Stockmann (following him about).	Give me my hat and stick.
Dr. Stockmann (in the same tone as before).	If you are the chief constable, let me tell you that I am the Mayor—I am the master of the whole town please understand!
Peter Stockmann.	Take off my hat, I tell you. Remember it is part of an official uniform.
Dr. Stockmann.	Pooh! Do you think the newly awakened lion-hearted people are going to be frightened by an official hat? There is going to be a revolution in the town tomorrow, let me tell you. You thought you could turn me out; but now I shall turn you out—turn you out of all your various offices. Do you think I cannot? Listen to me. I have triumphant social forces

> behind me. Hovstad and Billing will thunder in the "Peoples Messenger," and Aslaksen will take the field at the head of the whole Householders' Association—(240–241)

Act IV

Thomas has learned that those he thought supported him—Hovstad, Billing, Aslaksen—have abandoned him. But the ambition to vanquish Peter and serve in his stead still rules, and so he arranges to deliver the paper the *Messenger* has now refused to print in a hall provided by his friend the sea-captain Horster, all other venues having been closed to him by Peter and his associates. The crowd is not favorably disposed. Obedient to the wishes of the Mayor and self-interest of its staff, the *Messenger* has printed an article by Peter stating that Dr. Stockmann "is in the wrong" (246). Thomas attempts to read his article on the Baths. (The stage direction reads, "*Takes his* M.S. *out of his pocket*" [247]). However, Peter, who speaks first, asserts that Thomas's accounts of the pollution are "unreliable and exaggerated" (249). Anxious to avoid the accusation of responsibility for that pollution, he suggests that Thomas should not be permitted "to read or to comment on his proposed lecture" (249), and subsequently elicits cries of approval for himself and "catcalls" directed at Thomas when he notes "that the main result of the Medical Officer's proposals—apart from their constituting a vote of censure on the leading men of the town—would be to saddle the ratepayers with an unnecessary expenditure of at least some thousand pounds" (249–250). It is clear that Peter has won, at least for the moment, and that Thomas has lost the support of the multitude. The mayor's arrival elicits "I'm damned" from Billing (247). (McFarlane: "damn me.") And indeed, Thomas will be tempted again by his brother's intervention. The rejection by the citizenry soon to follow, which Peter engineers, does not diminish this "idealist's" egocentric certitude and sense of self-importance; it magnifies them.

Rather than deliver his prepared speech he intends, he says, to "impart [to his audience] a discovery of far wider scope than the trifling matter that our water-supply is poisoned and our medicinal Baths are standing on pestiferous soil" (252). He refers, he says, to "the discovery that all the sources of our moral life are poisoned and the whole fabric of our civic community is founded on the pestiferous soil of falsehood" (253). He then unwittingly provides an example of precisely the "falsehood" he has just condemned. He gives a falsified history of his travails completely omitting the envy of and animosity towards Peter that have motivated him throughout. This paean of self-glorification—perfectly consistent with his reigning life-lie—presents him as the most well-intentioned and public spirited of citizens, committed even in exile to the "good of the community" (253).

"But," he says, "yesterday … afternoon the eyes of my mind were opened wide" (253). He refers to the "colossal stupidity of the authorities," the incompetence, the destructiveness, the "priggishness" of the "leading men," such as his "brother, Peter—slow witted and hide bound in prejudice" (253–254). However, the authorities are no longer his primary concern. He directs his venom now at those citizens who have just rejected him. "The most dangerous enemy of truth and freedom among us is the compact majority," he says (253). "[I]t is the masses—this infernal compact majority—that poisons the sources of our moral life, and infects the ground we stand upon." Thomas represents himself as one of the very few "Übermenschen" distinguished from the "compact majority" by their perception of, and devotion to, new and revolutionary truths. "They are fighting for truths that are too newly-born into the world of consciousness to have any considerable number of people on their side yet" (256). "A normally constituted truth lives, let us say, as a rule seventeen or eighteen, or at most twenty years; seldom longer. But truths as aged as that are worn frightfully thin, and nevertheless it is only then that the majority recognizes them and recommends them to the community as wholesome moral nourishment" (256–257). Unfortunately for his thesis Thomas himself affords a perfect example of the persistence of the very oldest of truths—the preoccupation with self, the desire for omnipotence that led in the first instance to the biblical Expulsion and, both before and after events depicted in this drama, to Thomas's own expulsion from society.

Thomas failure to "reign" in his brother's stead leads this egotist to the inevitable conclusion that only "intellectually superior personalities" such as he are fit to rule (258). "Well damn me if ever I—" says Billing, identifying that presumption for the reader as still another instance of the Devil's work. (McFarlane: "Well I'll be damned.") Thomas's goals have metamorphosed completely, but not the "life lie" that defines him. This erstwhile champion of the liberal "compact majority" has become their enemy, and indeed the enemy of all mankind. Dr. Stockmann, guardian of the public health, has become an advocate for death rather than for life:

Dr. Stockmann
(with growing fervor). What does the destruction of a community matter if it lives on lies! It ought to be razed to the ground, I tell you! All who live by lies ought to be exterminated like vermin!

> You will end by infecting the whole country; you will bring about such a state of things that the whole country will deserve to be ruined. And if things come to that pass, I shall say from the bottom of my heart: Let the whole country perish, let all these people be exterminated! (262)

Thomas unwittingly condemns himself; for he is precisely one who "lives on lies." But Ibsen clearly means to include all mankind; for nearly all in this play are similarly afflicted.

Thomas's egotistical self-regard continues to grow, culminating in identification with a sort of anti-Christ, a being equal to Christ in stature, but antithetical in morality—a fitting evolution for one already in the clutches of the Father of Lies:

> *Dr. Stockmann*
> *(Raising his voice)*. You will hear more of this enemy of the people, before he shakes the dust off his shoes upon you! I am not so forgiving as a certain Person; I do not say: "I forgive you, for ye know not what ye do." (266)

Act V

The authorities and the crowd they govern are equally guilty of hypocrisy. As noted Ibsen speaks of universal failings of which the Stockmanns afford specific examples. The well-being of one's fellow man, of visitors to the Baths who will sicken and perhaps die, is no longer the concern of Thomas, of Peter, of the staff of the *Messenger*, or of the "compact majority." All save Thomas prefer to believe the life-lie stipulating the health-bestowing benefits of the polluted waters. Those who accuse Thomas of blasphemy are blasphemers themselves, indifferent to Christ's teaching: "Let he who is without sin cast the first stone." The stones that litter the floor of Thomas's study testify to that (267). Thomas's trousers are rent by a crowd "ready to tear the clothes off [his] back" (280)—an obvious reference to the disrobing of Christ and division of his garments (John 19.23–24). However, in this instance the event is comic not tragic, emphasizing the disparity between the egocentric, petty Thomas who thinks himself superior to, yet savior of, "his people," and the humble Savior Himself.

Thomas's egotism is undiminished, indeed exacerbated, by those acts of violence: "That the common herd should dare to make this attack on me, as if they were my equals—that is what I cannot, for the life of me, swallow!" (268). He proposes to leave the town and the country that have rejected him and set up again in the New World. Captain Horster, who could have transported him there on his ship, has lost his command in consequence of befriending Thomas, but says that if Thomas is "determined to go away," he has "thought of another plan" that would make this possible (273).

Before we can learn what it is, Peter Stockmann enters. He, too, tempts Thomas. Petra and Thomas are no longer employed, and the townspeople now refuse to become the doctor's patients. His family is again impoverished with no relief in sight. Peter offers an alternative, saying that if Thomas can see fit to "write a few words of regret, acknowledging [his] error" his position and income might in future be restored. "I would not do it," says Thomas, "if I had the devil and his dam on my back—! Never—never, I tell you!" (275). (McFarlane: "I wouldn't care if I had the devil himself *and* his old woman on my back. …" Italics in original.)

Thomas rejects his brother's offer precisely because it is his brother's offer. He must be superior, not inferior, to Peter. Peter, however, attributes his brother's obstinacy to the expectation of an inheritance from the wealthy Kiil. He tells Thomas not to count on that. Kiil could "alter his will any day he likes." Thomas replies, "But he won't do that, my dear Peter. The 'Badger' is much too delighted at my attack on you and your wise friends" (277). Peter responds by accusing his brother of deliberately condemning the management of the Baths to please the irascible Kiil:

> *Peter Stockmann.* I see that the whole thing was a combined manoeuvre on your part and his. These violent, reckless attacks that you have made against the leading men of the town, under the pretence that it was in the name of truth … were nothing else than the stipulated price for that vindictive old man's will … All is over between us. Your dismissal is irrevocable—we have a weapon against you now. (*Goes out*) (277)

Kiil, the next to enter, also offers reward for repudiation. He has purchased numerous shares in the Baths cheaply because of the rumors of pollution that have gotten about. The inheritance of Thomas's family is, he says, fully invested in the Baths' securities. Kiil's tannery is a major source of the pollution. Nonetheless he means "to live and die a clean man" without stain on his reputation (279). If Thomas repudiates his condemnation of the Baths and of the tannery the value of the stocks will rise and the future of Thomas's family, and of Thomas himself, will be assured. If he does not, Kiil will donate the securities to charity. Thomas has until two o' clock to decide.

Kill is clearly another tempter:

Dr. Stockmann
(advancing towards [Kiil]). To think you could do such a preposterous thing! Risking Katherine's money in this way, and putting me in such a horribly painful dilemma! When I look at you I think I see the devil himself—(280). (McFarlane. "When I look at you it's just like looking at the devil himself.")

And Thomas is tempted. He does not reject Kill's offer outright, but proposes to talk it over with his wife. Before he can do so Hovstad and Aslaksen enter. "What the devil!" Thomas says (280). Like Peter, they accuse Thomas of collusion with Kiil, asserting that Thomas condemned the baths to lower the price of its shares so that Kiil could make a killing, which he and Thomas would share. Thomas reacts violently, threatening them with force. "Where the devil is my stick?" he says, intending to drive them out (283); for they, too, are tempters. He tells his wife, that he now intends to remain in the town: "This is the field of battle—this is where the fight will be. This is where I shall triumph" (285).

Why does he change his mind? And what does he mean by "triumph"?

Had Thomas left after the controversy provoked by his talk—as he originally intended—he would have been able to regard himself (falsely) as a superior moral and intellectual being driven out by his duplicitous inferiors. But that was before the "opportunity" offered by Peter's, Aslaksen's and Hovstad's condemnation of his motives.

If Thomas remains and accepts Kiil's offer he will perhaps be able to correct, or at least improve, conditions at the Baths because of his connections with its principle stockholder who is also a chief source of the pollution. His critique of the Baths rescinded, the town will continue to flourish; and he and his family will be the recipients of his wife's substantial inheritance. However, his enemies will regard him, and see to it that others regard him, as a timeserver who had always the basest of motives. The egocentric need to be perceived as superior prohibits that recourse. If Thomas does not accept Kiil's offer and leaves he will demonstrate his moral superiority. The shares will go to charity and so Thomas cannot profit. But he will not have opportunity to vaunt it over those whom he despises and prefers to believe beneath him. And that is a pleasure this egotist cannot deny himself. By staying and rejecting the inheritance he confirms his moral superiority *and* is afforded endless opportunities to flaunt it before his critics. He will be able to circulate news of his "discovery" in nearby towns that have much to gain by the disclosure, which will insure the impoverishment of the now hated "compact majority" in his own town. He must remain if he is to accomplish and witness those developments. He proposes to begin his revelations and criticisms immediately: "Well, I think I have had a visit from every one of the devil's messengers to-day!" (McFarlane: "Well, if this hasn't been a hell of a day for callers, I don't know what is.") "But now I am going to sharpen my pen till they can feel its point; I shall steep it in venom and gall; I shall hurl my ink-pot at their heads!," he says (285). Believing he has triumphed over his tempters—in this passage he compares himself to Luther, who according to legend resisted the temptations the Devil and threw his inkpot at him to confirm it—he in fact succumbs to what is, for this egotist, the greatest temptation of all. By refusing to withdraw his warnings about the polluted Baths and eliminate so far as possible the source of pollution, he condemns his family to poverty and impoverishes his fellow citizens, all to maintain the blatantly false and incongruous fiction that he is the most truthful, noble and superior of beings.

It is likely, that Peter, Hovstad and Aslaksen have already spread the word that Thomas is a fraud. They will be condemned when it is discovered that the inheritance has gone to charity. Their other criticisms of Thomas will then be questioned. Sooner or later the malignant character of the Baths will become apparent—sooner rather than later if Thomas is able to get the word out to neighboring communities. And so he will be vindicated on both counts. He, not his brother, will be the final victor. To achieve and savor that victory, Thomas must remain.

The pollution of the Baths affects only the body. Thomas's affliction is more serious. Egotism has infected his very soul, spreading ever farther and deeper. When his wife Katherine points out that without any source of income his family will be hard-pressed to afford even food he replies "That gives me very little concern" (286–287). Katherine will simply have to "pinch and save a bit"! Kiil offers a more accurate assessment: "it will be exactly as if you were to flay broad strips of skin from Katherine's body, and Petra's and the boys'" (279). His image recalls the torments of the damned, and indeed Thomas has consigned his family to penury and hunger in a mirrored Underworld that reflects only himself. "[T]he strongest man in the world is he who stands most alone." Thomas, the singular, extraordinary Übermensch is alone worthy of worship and exaltation. He again compares himself to Christ; however his twelve disciples will be twelve street urchins whom he proposes to school in his doctrines (287). They will necessarily confirm his egotistic belief in his supremacy.

Petra's concluding cry of "Father!" as she "encouragingly" clasps his hands, suggests that for that misguided atheist, Thomas, unwitting disciple of the Father of Lies, because himself the father of lies, has replaced the very Godhead, God the Father (288). Thomas is indeed an enemy of the people. But then so are the other personae in Ibsen's profound tragicomedy.

Notes

1. Hermann J. Weigand, *Modern Ibsen*, 102.
2. Edmund Gosse in McFarlane, *Henrik Ibsen: A Critical Anthology*, 119.
3. Robert Brustein, "Ibsen and Revolt," 119.
4. Thomas F. Van Laan, 96.
5. Eric Bentley in Fjelde, *Critical Essays*, 16.
6. Thomas F. Van Laan, 97.
7. Thomas F. Van Laan, 113.
8. Richard Hornby in Van Laan, 98.
9. Inge-Stina Ewbank in Lyons, *Critical Essays*, 79.
10. Daniel Haakonsen in Lyons, *Critical Essays*, 215–216.
11. Richard Hornby, *Patterns*, 151; italics in original.
12. Michael Meyer in Matos, "Choleric Fictions," 356.
13. Arne Garborg in Thomas F. Van Laan, 114, fn. 26.
14. Hermann J. Weigand, *Modern Ibsen*, 103.
15. James McFarlane in *Henrik Ibsen: Four Major Plays*, xii.

References

All parenthetical page citations in this text are from *Eleven Plays of Henrik Ibsen*, ed. B. A. Cerf, D. S. Klopfer. New York: *The Modern Library*, 1935. Translators not given but those of plays discussed in this volume appear to be R. Farquharson Sharp (*Ghosts*, *An Enemy of the People*), Edmund Gosse and William Archer (*The Master Builder*, *Hedda Gabler*), and William Archer (*The Wild Duck*). I found those older translations satisfactory for my purposes. In the few cases where translation appeared to be an issue I have appended parallel citations from *The Oxford Ibsen*. (McFarlane, James Walter, ed. and trans. *The Oxford Ibsen*, 8 vols. London: Oxford University Press, 1962.)

Brustein, Robert. "Ibsen and Revolt." *The Tulane Review* 7, no. 1 (Autumn 1962): 113–154.

Fjelde, Rolf, ed. *Ibsen: A Collection of Critical Essays*. Englewood Cliffs, NJ: Prentice-Hall, 1965.

Hornby, Richard. *Patterns in Ibsen's Middle Plays*. Lewisburg: Bucknell University Press, 1981.

Lyons, Charles R., ed. *Critical Essays on Henrik Ibsen*. Boston: G. K. Hall & Co., 1987.

Matos, Timothy Carlo. "Choleric Fictions: Epidemiology, Medical Authority, and *An Enemy of the People*." *Modern Drama* 51, no. 3 (Fall 2008): 353–368.

McFarlane, James, ed. *Henrik Ibsen: A Critical Anthology*. Harmondsworth, Middlesex, England: Penguin Books, 1970.

McFarlane, James, and Jens Arup, trans. *Henrik Ibsen, Four Major Plays*. *Oxford World's Classics*. Oxford, England: Oxford University Press, 2008.

McFarlane, James, trans. *Henrik Ibsen, An Enemy of the People, The Wild Duck, Rosmerholm*. *Oxford World's Classics*. Oxford, England: Oxford University Press, 1999.

Van Laan, Thomas F. "Generic Complexity in Ibsen's 'An Enemy of the People.'" *Comparative Drama* 20, no. 2 (Summer 1986): 95–114.

Weigand, Hermann J. *The Modern Ibsen*. New York: Henry Holt & Co., 1925.

· 3 ·

DE PROFUNDIS

Werle.	There are people in the world who dive to the bottom the moment they get a couple of slugs in their body and never come to the surface again.
	....
Ekdal.	[the wild duck] was only wounded.
Gregers.	Ah! She got a couple of slugs in her body, I suppose.
Hjalmar.	Yes, two or three.
Hedvig.	She was hit under the wing, so that she couldn't fly.
Gregers.	And I suppose she dived to the bottom, eh?
Ekdal (sleepily, in a thick voice).	Of course. Always do that, wild ducks do. They shoot to the bottom as deep as they can get, sir—and bite themselves fast in the tangle and seaweed—and all the devil's own mess that grows down there. And they never come up again.
	....
Hedvig.	... whenever I come to realize suddenly—in a flash—what is in [the garret], it always seems to me that the whole room and everything in it should be called "the depths of the sea."
	....
Gregers to Hjalmar.	You have dived down and bitten yourself fast in the undergrowth.

Prefatory

One does not have to look far to find critics mystified or put off by the symbolism of Ibsen's wounded bird. Arnold Bennet thought Ibsen's symbolism "simply deplorable."[1] For Weigand "the wild duck symbolism" is "tomfoolery"[2] inserted simply to demonstrate Gregers' "penchant for wallowing in symbols."[3] Hornby observes "In terms of the play's action … it seems silly or bizarre."[4] For T. R. Henn "the recurrence of the symbolism grows wearisome."[5] Toril Moi regards the wild duck as an instance of Gregers' "bizarrely symbolic language."[6]

`James McFarlane and others rightly disagree. "[N]o genuinely dramatic reaction is possible without [the symbol]," McFarlane says. "It concentrates, it holds together a number of otherwise separate things, it permits that density by which art distinguishes itself from the more diffuse nature of life, it helps to compose the drama."[7] Northam notes "the symbol's capacity for positive growth": "Out of the action of the play, and inseparable in development from that, emerges the most poignant and poetic implication as the full potency of the image is developed."[8]

As our epigraphs indicate Gregers is neither the first nor the only one in the drama to allude to the metaphorical implications of the wild duck. It is central to the action, contributing directly to its climax, the death of Hedvig. To regard the symbol simply as the invention and obsession of an impractical "transcendental idealist" ignorant of, or indifferent to the implications of his behavior is to trivialize an image to which Ibsen—by titling his play as he does, by seeing to it that not one but several characters refer to it directly or indirectly, and by having its material embodiment contribute so significantly to the plot—obviously attributes great significance.

Birds have long symbolized the human soul. Ibsen employs this familiar metaphor in *The Master Builder* (predatory Hilde compares herself to a bird of prey [351]). His wild duck represents souls crippled by circumstance, or more broadly by "life." They react by rejecting painful truths, substituting instead comforting illusions, or what the physician Relling calls "life-lies" (796). Ibsen figures this as descent from the world of light, which, as in *Ghosts*, he associates with truth, to the confinement of dark undersea depths that represent ignorance of self and of others. There his crippled souls, confusing what is life-giving with what is death-dealing, cling to the fatal illusions that sustain them as the wounded duck does to the seaweed to avoid the hunter above. Like the bird, they are fearful of returning to the potentially hazardous, painful "upper" sunlit world. Those souls, too, "never come up again."

The metaphor posits a prior state of relative freedom before one's descent into darkness. As the wild duck was once free, so were Ibsen's protagonists. This is obviously true of the Ekdals, once financially well off and admired before their "descent," and in particular of old Ekdal, famous hunter of bears, who once roamed the forests in search of game. But all protagonists in this drama are victims. In a letter to his publisher Ibsen noted the "manifold failings" of "the persons in this play"; and that is clearly the case.[9]

Ibsen's lighting reflects the relationship of light and dark to truth and falsehood. As Ronald Peacock observes, "light is … used by Ibsen, not only to indicate the passage of time, but also as a symbolic accompaniment to the action."[10] Ibsen himself wrote "I attach much importance to the lighting in this play. I wanted it to correspond to the basic mood prevailing in each of the five acts."[11]

When we first encounter the Ekdals at home it is evening. The simulated wood where old Ekdal now hunts is illumined only by the moon. Much of the garret is in darkness. The conversation in the foreground, characterized by constant evasion of the truth, is as "unreal" as the synthetic forest. The revelation of truths that temporarily obliterate the false world of the Ekdals is prefigured in Act III by the sunlight that illuminates pseudo forest and garret. During the sunlit morning and early afternoon walk which occurs between acts III and IV Gregers conveys to Hjalmar the truths—as he perceives them—of Werle's interventions in the Ekdal's affairs. The gathering twilight of act IV is an appropriate setting for the revelation of the illusions entertained by Hjalmar and Gregers that contribute to Hedvig's death. The unique fusion of truth and falsehood, of real and unreal in act V, such as the juxtaposition of Hedvig's genuine anguish with Hjalmar's pretentious, self-serving "agony," determines in part the half-darkness of Ibsen's "*Cold, grey morning light*," the "*Wet snow [that] lies upon the large panes of the sloping roof*" obscuring the daylight, the garret so dark "you can scarcely see where you're going" (798). Neither light nor darkness prevails, nor does reality or illusion. With the death of Hedvig, Hjalmar and Gregers, who both contributed to that tragedy, become aware of the awful consequences of their surrender to the unreal. Hjalmar cruelly rejected the one person who loved him unconditionally, and Gregers insisted upon the unnecessary sacrifice, motivated by that misconceived rejection, that led to her death. Their confrontation with actuality is, however, temporary. For Hjalmar, Hedvig's death "will become but a petty theme for declamation" (812). Gregers conceals his instrumental role from the others and inwardly absolves himself by arguing that the girl's sacrifice will redeem the irredeemable Hjalmar. Ibsen's semi-darkness suggests both their exposure to, and retreat from, painful truths.

The equivalence of light and truth implies that blindness, like darkness, signifies ignorance. Those threatened by it have succumbed to illusion. As Mary McCarthy notes "blindness is a metaphor for the state of darkened self-deception in which the little family lives."[12] All references in the drama to fear of the light, to imperfect vision, to one's reluctance to see have a related significance. The duck itself, which has adapted completely to its new surroundings, is obviously blind to the fact that it is no longer free.

Drunkenness is a related motif. Gregers' deceased mother and Hjalmar's father, Relling the physician and Molvik the theological student were, or are, alcoholics who prefer the illusory solace of drink to painful awareness of reality.

The photograph accurately represents imperfect reality. Retouching creates the illusion of eliminating its flaws; and that is the occupation of Hjalmar and family. They "retouch" their difficult, unsatisfactory lives as they do the photographs they take. "Retouching" transforms the vain, ineffectual, indolent Hjalmar into someone worthy of respect and admiration. "From the beginning it can be seen that the members of the Ekdal family, especially Hjalmar, have a tendency to evade the unpleasant truths: to retouch the reality, or in Goldman's word, '*to make the picture come out right*—to adjust reality so that it 'looks good''."[13] The primary instance of this metamorphosis is of course the artificial wood in the Ekdal garret. Old Ekdal has created an alternate cosmos, "a sort of world by itself" (749) where he can again become the great hunter he once was. There time, which brought with it imprisonment and shame, "has come to a standstill" at the preferred, vanished past (749), an event symbolized by the broken clock in the garret's shadowed depths. Reality in its entirety is "retouched."

The false, or falsified, map boundaries that led to old Ekdal's downfall afford an early instance of "retouching" and its negative consequences. As he aptly remarks, "The woods avenge themselves" (810): "redrawing" or "retouching" reality exacts its toll. That is the unifying thesis of the play. (The Norwegian *uefterrettelige* can mean "unreliable" as well as "false." Werle asserts that old Ekdal deliberately falsified the maps. Those who sentenced him to prison obviously agreed (711). Gregers's objection that old Ekdal "seems to have been very much in the dark as to what he was doing" is clearly an attempt to blame Werle for the old man's misfortune. As I hope to demonstrate, it is an aspect of Gregers's "blindness" and hence suspect. Werle's assertion of innocence is equally questionable. In fact all participants, father, son, and, as we later learn, old Ekdal, who continues to secretly wear the uniform his error or malfeasance have deprived him of, reinterpret or "retouch" this event as it suits them. We shall observe that Hjalmar does not question the suspect and illusory when it confers an advantage. In such cases "retouching" amounts to ignoring inconvenient facts. One is blind to or overlooks the flaws of the real. Old Ekdal resembles his son in this. It was his responsibility and Werle's to research the "unreliable" map, if it was in fact unreliable. But it was more profitable to accept its false or "retouched" representation of reality.)

Act I

The symbolic associations of light and darkness determine the division of the stage into dimly lit front room and brilliantly lit back rooms. Ibsen's arrangement signifies that falsehood, not truth, will be most visible in this drama—will occupy the foreground as it were. The businessman Werle refuses to acknowledge his multiple betrayals—of wife, of child, of partner, of partner's son and wife. Ibsen represents this avoidance of truth as approaching blindness that necessitates retreat from the brilliantly lit rear rooms where Werle entertains his lackeys and hangers on to the shadowed study in the foreground. Shabby, bewigged old Ekdal, who "*appears from the right, in the inner room*," is revealed in all his inadequacies by the same brilliant background light. As Northam notes, "The pretense is blatant and pathetic."[14]

Beneath the strong light Bertha Sörby engages in blind man's buff with her long-time acquaintances, the chamberlains. Werle expects to marry Sörby whom he will sorely need when blind. He plans to move with her to his Höidal mines located in a remote, isolated wooded area. Just as he has always striven to obscure his questionable actions, so the marriage to this woman of easy virtue is to occur there, out of public view. And there he will be able to conceal his blindness from others as all in this drama conceal theirs. Another motive for his move, surely, is to prevent the vivacious, pleasure loving Bertha "who can always find a loop-hole" (707) from betraying him—all too easy when blindness supervenes. Gregers accurately points out to him that the game of blind man's buff—tasteless and cruel on the part of Mrs. Sörby, who is well aware of Werle's infirmity—foreshadows that event. (Northam characterizes it as "an unpleasant innuendo of what is likely to happen when blindness comes."[15]) Sörby's flirtatious game-playing reflects the truth Werle perceives but prefers not to recognize: self preservation, not affection, motivates this woman who, like the chamberlains, is dependent upon Werle's largesse, and who, like them, perceives life as "a struggle for existence" (706). Charles Lyons assertion that Werle is "The one character that seems to see reality as it is …"[16] is clearly unwarranted. So is Robert Raphael's characterization of "wise old Werle" who, "like some God," has made it possible for the Ekdals to create their own paradisiacal refuge.[17] Werle's reluctance to accept responsibility for his misdeeds, his incipient blindness, his forced retreat from the bright light of the background emblematic of truth to the dimly lit study in the foreground, arena of self-deception and misrepresentation, indicate that he is as deluded as the rest.

Old Ekdal's appearance on the very day Hjalmar is invited to Werle's lavish banquet cannot be accidental. Perhaps he hoped to see his son again in the elegant setting familiar to both before his disgrace. Whatever his expectations, the reality must have been a terrible blow. It is not surprising that he seeks solace in alcohol as soon as he returns home. His son refuses to look at him, to acknowledge him—refuses to acknowledge the spiritual and physical impoverishment of the father he professes to love. This refusal to look, to apprehend unpleasant truths, to wish them away, is characteristic of Hjalmar. "Don't come near me Hedvig! Keep far away, I cannot bear to see you" he says to her after he learns, or thinks he learns, she is Werle's child (787).

The sudden silence of the guests who gather in "*a group … talking softly*" suggests that some at least surmise the identity of the bewigged old man—rumored to have been betrayed by Werle—who significantly averts his eyes (708), but suppress this knowledge for fear of offending their host. Falsification and deceit are the predominant motifs, qualifying the actions of all gathered in the dimly-lit study. There Werle rejects Gregers' legitimate accusations of malfeasance and infidelity as the products of an overwrought imagination. In fact Werle bears the burden of unacknowledged guilt. The "*dejected*" response of this ruthless materialist—critical of his deceased wife's religiosity—to the unlucky "thirteen at table" indicates that notwithstanding his protestations of innocence he fears retribution for "things ill done and done to others' harm" (698).

Hjalmar's account of his past depicts Werle as his philanthropic benefactor. We know this to be false. Does Hjalmar himself really believe it? He is of course aware that Gina had once been Werle's housekeeper. Is it possible that this formerly close friend of the family was completely ignorant of Werle's reputation for seducing his female help? Jensen, the hired waiter at Werle's party, was aware of it, as were others in the town: "Is it true, what folks say, that [Bertha Sörby and Werle are] very good friends, eh? … I've heard tell as he's been a lively customer in his day" (697–698).

Hjalmar later professes to discover for the first time that Hedvig's weak eyes signify she is Werle's child. There, too, one detects possible suppression of an unpalatable truth. Gregers remarks that his father's eyes "have always been weak" (714). This must have been known to the son of his former partner. Hjalmar is aware that Werle, like Hedvig, is losing his sight; he overhears Mrs. Sörby and Werle talking about it (705). Old Ekdal knows of Werle's long-failing vision. He tells Gregers in Hjalmar's presence that the duck was not killed outright because "your father's sight is not very good now." (736–737). It should have been evident to Hjalmar that Werle kept in touch with Gina after she left his service; for Hjalmar learned of the availability of a room at her mother's "little eating-house" from him (704). The dates of Hedvig's conception and birth, the ambiguity with which Gina deliberately shrouds the duration of their marriage (cf.732 & 773), suggests that Hjalmar long had reasons to suspect Werle might have been Gina's former lover and Hedvig's father. But if he did, this dependent, indolent individual, for whom truth is largely what he prefers it to be (witness his retelling of events at Werle's dinner when he returns home), would have suppressed the knowledge. Otherwise he could not "in good conscience" have accepted Werle's financial support, or permitted his father to be employed by Werle. He had some assistance in this from old Ekdal who told him, perhaps to insure his income from Werle for copying, that his mother had weak eyes (731).

Hjalmar's indifference to the family finances leads one to the same conclusion. Although necessarily aware that Gina must have sufficient income to cover his expensive tastes and frequent entertaining, Hjalmar refrains from asking her for an accounting which might have revealed their indebtedness to Werle. He suspects something is amiss (771), but would rather not know. He acts only after Gregers forces the issue. Hjalmar is clearly capable of such self-deception when his own indolent life-style is at risk. In the last act he repairs and accepts—ostensibly for his father, but of course for himself—Werle's torn deed of gift *after* concluding that Hedvig is Werle's daughter (804).

Werle's possible role in old Ekdal's tragedy is apparent to Gregers and suspected by others. Werle notes that "It is thanks to [Ekdal] that I—yes *I*—have had a kind of slur cast on my reputation." His concern not to encourage suspicions of guilt by being overly generous to the Ekdals suggests that those suspicions still pursue him. The three seedy chamberlains, friends of Bertha Sörby, who is herself suspect because willing to live in sin more or less openly, suggest the sort of guests Werle is able to attract. They are evidence that polite society is still suspicious of him, notwithstanding his insistence that "the whole story

[was] forgotten long ago" (711). As Northam notes, "If the host (and hostess) are to be judged by their company the verdict can hardly be entirely favorable."[18] Yet, throughout his conversation with Gregers Hjalmar assumes that old Ekdal alone was guilty. (*Hjalmar to Gregers*. "Your father was within an ace of being drawn into that—well, that terrible business" [701]). He praises Werle for his compassionate interest in and generosity to the Ekdals. Surely self-interest as well as politeness is at work here. One does not want to kill the goose that lays the golden eggs, even if it entails betrayal of one's parent.

Hjalmar professes to learn that Werle was responsible for his father's ruin only after his long walk and conversation with Gregers. Although the conversation occurs offstage we can reconstruct the relevant parts. Gregers has told him guilt compels Werle to pay old Ekdal far more than he is worth. Hence, he later asks Gina: "Is it the case that father is very liberally paid for the copying he does for Mr. Werle?" (771). Hjalmar could have obtained this information from his wife at any time; but it might have put an end to his feasting and entertaining, and so he did not ask.

Werle, who knows Hjalmar has long had reasons to suspect him of betraying both father and son, has a low opinion of him. He probably believes Hjalmar has suppressed the truth for the sake of financial gain. This is suggested by his conversation with Gregers in act III. Gregers argues that Hjalmar will welcome a truthful account of his situation; Werle doubts it (764). He cannot give his reasons to Gregers, without admitting he is guilty of the wrongs done the Ekdals, and may be Hedvig's father. And so he offers only generalities in an attempt to dissuade his son from his "mission" of retrieving the Ekdals from the depths of Ibsen's metaphoric sea.

Hjalmar has but one actual invention to his credit—the net that blurs the connection between unreal and real worlds, transforming the second into an extension of the first, just as Hjalmar himself does. Photography—absent "retouching"—accurately depicts the real. It is, therefore appropriate that his other "invention" which is to revolutionize photography, is still-born. Consistent with this, practical Gina takes the photographs. Her spouse confines himself to retouching.

Ibsen wrote that "This part [Hjalmar] must absolutely not be acted with anything like parody in the expression; nor with the slightest trace of awareness in the actor that there is anything at all comic in his utterances."[19] To portray Hjalmar as a buffoon would be to interpose another consciousness constantly evaluating him between the character and the audience, defeating the authenticity, the "realism" that was Ibsen's objective. Hjalmar and the others live a "life-lie" of which they are not consciously aware. Therefore the absurdity of his actions and statements cannot be evident to him, to Gina or to Hedvig. Their ignorance would be difficult to accept were he patently ridiculous. He is not to know that he is a fraud, nor are they. Hedvig's death would otherwise be trivialized, deprived of the seriousness and significance it deserves as a consequence of the self-deceit that blinds these individuals to the truth.

Gregers, too, is not to know what actually motivates him. He is to see himself as an idealist, who seeks only to enlighten the "wounded" and liberate them from their submarine prison. In fact, his primary, if suppressed, motivation is hatred of his father, whom he blames for his own weaknesses and betrayals and hopes to discredit. His attempt to "redeem" Hjalmar is inextricably fused (or confused) with this very different motive. (Compare Northam: "This seems to be the true motive-power behind Gregers, this hatred for his father."[20]). We will consider the evidence in due course. Here I need cite only a few relevant remarks:

Werle.	Gregers—I believe there is no one in the world you detest as you do me.
Gregers (softly).	I have seen you at too close quarters (716).
	....
Gregers.	'Gregers'—and then 'Werle' after it; did you ever imagine anything so hideous? ... I feel I should like to spit upon the fellow that answers to that name (739).
	....
Werle.	Is it I, then, that have crippled your mind, Gregers?
Gregers.	You have crippled my whole life (764).

Gregers here compares himself to the wild duck, "crippled" by Werle. Fear and hatred of his father caused him, he says, to retreat to the Höidal mines, an underworld symbolically comparable to the depths sought out by the wounded duck. And there he remained until Werle called him forth. His interest in the Ekdals and in Hjalmar stems partly from the perceived likeness of their experience to his: they too are wounded victims of Werle. And that evokes and confirms his hatred of his father. He tells Werle, "When I look back upon your past I seem to see a battle-field with shattered lives on every hand" (717).

A summary of the bare facts supports this interpretation of Gregers' motives. For seventeen years he has been at Höidal. During that time he never once saw his father or, apparently, desired to see him. When they do meet, he severs all connection with Werle, telling him that he never wants to see him again. He accuses Werle of immoral and criminal behavior involving his deceased wife and the Ekdals. He refuses Werle's offer of a partnership. He later rejects the share of Werle's estate that will be legally his when Werle remarries.

Of course one can hate one's father and still be committed to Truth and to the Ideal as Gregers claims to be. But in this instance the commitment has a singular focus. Gregers' pursuit of Truth and promulgation of the Ideal are exclusively devoted to the revelation of Werle's wrongs. They are fully compatible and consistent with hatred. Hatred is an ignoble motivation, and so better represented—to oneself and to others—as concern for Truth and the Ideal. For Gregers to acknowledge he is compelled by hatred would be to admit that Werle, from whom he obviously wishes to distance himself, still determined his actions, and that they, too, were corrupt.

Hence, when Gregers speaks to Werle of his newly discovered "mission" (717) he refers not to the animosity that actually motivates him, but to the enlightenment and redemption of the Ekdals, especially Hjalmar (764). Note, however, that Gregers, who has not contacted his "best and only friend" for seventeen years, resolves to save him and his family only *after* he concludes that his father has invited him down to lend respectability to his illicit affairs (716). Gregers correctly believes that for the sake of his future wife and himself Werle wishes to create the false illusion of a compassionate husband who was always faithful to his deceased wife, and the equally false illusion of a "happy" family where there was and is none. Reconciliation with his son will send that message. Gregers refuses to play along. He decides instead to deprive the father he detests of the respectability he craves. The truth, which he intends to disclose to Hjalmar, will reveal Werle to be a self-seeking opportunist who betrayed wife and partner, and callously used the family of the man he ruined to conceal his own sins. Hjalmar affords Gregers the opportunity to disseminate those truths and turn Hjalmar, who professes to admire Werle, against him, and others in future against him. He becomes the means to an unexpressed, unconscious or semi-conscious end.

The hatred that motivates Gregers throughout is evident in his subsequent threat to tell Werle about Bertha Sörby's past affair with Relling. He says to Sörby "Are you not in the least afraid that I may let my father know about this old friendship" (779). Redemption of the Ekdals is obviously not his objective here, but rather a wish to poison the relationship between future husband and wife, and perhaps deprive his father of a companion who, when blind, he will sorely need. "Truthfulness" is merely a convenient excuse.

In the dimly-lit study we also gain insight into the cowardice of this proponent of the "ideal," which he obviously thinks entails heroic confrontation with truth, however unpleasant. We learn that he abandoned the mother he claims to love and whose memory he professes to cherish. He was away at Höidal during the critical final year of her illness, when "she broke down and came to such a pitiful end" (713), and apparently did not return for her funeral (704). Although aware of Hjalmar's "fall"—for he knew his "best and only friend" had taken up photography to survive (702)—he avoided all contact with him for seventeen years. Gregers subsequently admits (in act III) that he "ought to have taken a stand against [Werle] when the trap was set for lieutenant Ekdal. [He] ought to have cautioned him; for [he] had a misgiving as to what was in the wind." He did not intervene. Fear of his father, who "crippled him," prevented it. It is clear that he blames Werle, not himself, for his failure to act and for old Ekdal's tragedy. "[I]t's thanks to you that I am continually haunted and harassed by a guilty conscience," he says (764). As we shall observe, his cowardly refusal to take responsibility for Hedvig's death is consistent with those earlier omissions.

Given Gregers' profound, long-standing hatred of his father, it is likely that his former efforts to interest Werle's cottagers in "the claim of the ideal" also figured as an attempt to discredit Werle. Gregers probably sought to convince the miners they were being exploited by a scoundrel who had unfairly shifted criminal blame to his partner. Relling tells us that the attempt failed. But the son's hatred endured, and so led to a second attempt when opportunity offered.

Gregers is ugly. (*Gina*: "Is Gregers as ugly as ever?" *Hjalmar*: "Well, he's not very much to look at" [722]). He does not expect to marry (703). He has no friends save Hjalmar. He is incompetent in practical matters—consider the mess he makes of his room when he attempts to light the fire (742), and his failure to convert the cottagers at Höidal to his conception of the "ideal." He is clearly inferior to his father—seducer of women, successful businessman, surrounded by seeming admirers who depend upon him for "survival."

Hjalmar is still good looking, ("he was handsome ... a shop girls dream of manly beauty" says Relling [795]). Gregers notices this. "[Y]our outer man is in first-rate condition," he says (701). Hjalmar has a wife, a family, and friends, is more or less content with his lot, and claims to be the creator of a significant "invention." Unhappy, solitary, ugly, ineffectual Gregers has cause to envy both parent and friend and—unconsciously—wish them ill.

Gregers alone has heard Werle's comparison of the Ekdals to a wounded wild duck (711). The animal reminds him of, and symbolizes for him, his father's responsibility for their ruin, Werle's indifference to the consequences, and the Ekdals retreat into fantasy. He believes that if Hedvig and her family are to free themselves from Werle's grasp they must not only reject all financial aid from him, but also rid themselves of the creature that symbolizes and facilitates their self-imposed captivity. A marriage founded upon lies must be replaced by one founded upon truth. Those are Gregers' conscious motives; but they are not determinative. His suggestion that the Ekdals reject Werle's financial aid and that Hedvig kill her beloved duck are unconsciously motivated by hatred of his father. Nothing of Werle's is to remain. Werle must be obliterated. His comparison of the family to a wounded, drowning bird must be shown to be false. The need to sacrifice the duck becomes all the more urgent if we assume that the childless, wifeless, lonely Gregers is attracted to the adolescent Hedvig, apparently the only female, save his mother, who ever expressed an interest in him, and with whom he appears to have an instinctive rapport. For one as ugly as Gregers her deteriorating vision is clearly an asset. Hedvig's devotion to the duck becomes in Gregers' mind devotion to Werle, and that is unacceptable.

Such is the condition of nearly all in the drama. Nearly all occupy the shadowy foreground of the stage as it were, where "retouching" and the unconscious rule. Nearly all prefer illusion to reality. Relling's brief encounter with Bertha Sörby, which culminates in his decision to drown his sorrows in drink, is unrelated to the main action but necessary to prove that even this wise physician is afflicted with the universal "sickness," the "blindness," that prevents one from clearly perceiving difficult, condemnatory truths—in Relling's case the fact that he is an alcoholic who has "frittered away all that was good in him" (779).

The others are as willfully blind. Molvik accepts Relling's life-lie that he is a daemonic, and therefore not responsible for his actions. His response to Hedvig's death, "The child is not dead, but sleepeth," allies him with others who "retouch" reality (811). Gina has for fourteen years concealed her affair with Werle and the knowledge that he might be Hedvig's father. She claims to have "almost forgotten" those critical events that might threaten her marriage (773). She has long concealed the generous income old Ekdal receives from Werle which, had Hjalmar learned of it, surely would have raised troubling questions. She provides the material and emotional support for, and so perpetuates and participates in, Hjalmar's illusions and those of old Ekdal. Werle, who denies all guilt, confirms it by bestowing a substantial income for life upon those who have suffered at his hands. Hjalmar's unshakable self regard, encouraged by his family, is completely without foundation. And Gregers cloaks his hatred in benevolence. All are "wounded" inhabitants of the lightless depths who prefer the "life-lie" to truth.

The victim of their collective illusions, Hedvig, is perhaps the sole exception. But even she finds it necessary to retreat to the imaginary world of literature, of make-believe, to avoid the painful reality of which she is becoming increasingly aware. Whether she is the child of Hjalmar or of Werle is never settled. And that is as it should be. Hjalmar is as blind in his own way as Werle is in his. Hedvig's failing vision—which represents the inveterate habit of avoiding or "retouching" truth, and which is appropriately exacerbated by the act of retouching—could have been "inherited" from either. We may assume that until recently this innocent regarded the familial life-lies as truths. But, as Relling notes (777), adolescence has brought with it a new awareness. She is no longer completely content to reside in the depths of the "sea." And so we find her midway between uncritical acceptance and disappointment, manifest, for example, in her notion that the garret is in effect "undersea" and her recent interest in the game of "house-on-fire" (777). The latter clearly reveals an incipient, unacknowledged desire to destroy the unreal environment that imprisons her.

Act II

Hence, we find her in the second act "*sitting on the sofa, with her hands shading her eyes and her thumbs in her ears reading a book*" (718). Hedvig has "inherited" the disposition to shut out, neither to see nor hear, unpleasant realities. However, in this instance the impulse is directed against the life-lies that surround her. She prefers the illusions of literature—which are at least plainly and confessedly illusions—to the "realistic" illusions of the Ekdal household. Her concern that she have "some good news" to tell Hjalmar reveals her growing perception of the necessity for the life-lie and of its inadequacy (721). Her father must be continuously cosseted, favored, fed with delicacies to "cheer him up" and so prevent conscious awareness of his inferior, unsatisfactory status.

Nor is the artificial forest sufficient for old Ekdal. Act II reveals his need for the constant support of alcohol. Of course he pretends not to drink, and Gina and Hedvig pretend not to notice that he does drink. Hjalmar contributes to the pretense when he gives a false account of his behavior at Werle's. Old Ekdal, who noticed that his son pretended not to see him, pretends not to have noticed; and Hjalmar pretends not to have seen him pretend. The division between illusory forest in the background and domestic scene in the foreground diminishes. Foreground becomes almost as unreal as background, a fact Ibsen later emphasizes by having Hjalmar "invent" a net enclosure that permits the doors to the forest to remain open some of the time (745) allowing the illusory forest in the background to become almost a continuation of the foreground.

Into this eminently false setting comes Gregers, exponent of destructive "truths," knocking on the door "*almost immediately after*" Hjalmar exclaims "here dwells my happiness" (729). Gregers has ignored Hjalmar's express wish to meet elsewhere. He needs to observe the family at close hand if he is to "enlighten" his friend and so rip from his father the veil of respectability. And the visit is indeed worthwhile. Gregers learns that Hedvig is going blind; and that it is hereditary. His startled reaction (731) indicates he suspects she may be Werle's child. He asks about Hedvig's age, and its relationship to the date of Hjalmar's marriage. Hjalmar has been married 15 years (or is it 14? [731–732]). Hedvig is fourteen; but as Gregers observes she is "pretty tall for her age." The implication is that she may have been conceived before Hjalmar's marriage and thus may be Werle's daughter. Gina "*becomes attentive, looks at him* "(732); for she correctly suspects a hidden agenda.

Gregers then attempts to recall to old Ekdal and his family the old man's life before his trial and imprisonment (733). All must be reminded of what Werle's betrayal has cost them. He invites Ekdal to return with him to Höidal and again enjoy the freedom once his; but to no avail. He has not reckoned with the satisfaction Ekdal derives from his contrived forest, which has become equal or superior to the real thing in his eyes (v.796). Like the others he resembles the wild duck, which has not only "adjusted" but thrives in captivity (737). He, too, has "forgotten [his] natural wild life."

Gregers now perceives how completely the Ekdals are committed to illusion. His intent to expose them to the "truth," by which he means exclusively the evil done them by his father, will be more difficult than he had assumed. Rather than stay in a hotel as he had intended (729) he proposes to take a room let by the Ekdals, the better to insert himself into their lives. Gina fears Gregers knows more about the past than she wishes disclosed, and also worries that Werle, who provides significant income, may be offended by their friendship with the son who has rejected him, and so tries unsuccessfully to dissuade him.

Gregers resorts to the metaphor of the wild duck to suggest his new-found mission, telling the Ekdals he would like to be a clever dog able to retrieve such wounded birds from the ooze where they have bitten fast (739). He refers especially to Hjalmar, who, he thinks, has also retreated from light to darkness and now inhabits the depths of a miasmal swamp where there is only "dullness, oppression, gloom" (775). Hjalmar and Gina do not perceive his deeper, metaphorical, meaning; but Hedvig, who is beginning to sense—if not to understand—how committed her family is to illusion observes that Gregers "meant something quite different by that" (740).

Act III

It is daylight, an indication that a revelation is at hand. Gregers has managed to filthy his room in an unsuccessful attempt to light his stove. His incompetence prefigures the "mess" he soon makes of the Ekdal family's affairs by his intervention. It reveals his inability to anticipate the practical consequences of his acts. And it gives some insight into his former life at Höidal. This champion of self-reliance, who, as we soon perceive, would have the Ekdals renounce all income from Werle, must have had "at the very minimum … a woman to cook and clean and make the fires for him,"[21] whose salary was directly or indirectly furnished by the father he despised. Almost certainly his servant or servants came from the miners' class that Gregers tried and failed to convince of their unhealthy dependence upon his father. It is not surprising that they ignored his advice. More importantly, the filth is an allusion to hell, to the presence of evil—manifest symbolically as the Devil, Father of Lies, whose passage Ibsen associates with the sooty residue of Gregers' fire. In that dark underworld, deeper than the muddy bottom of Ibsen's metaphoric sea, this envious, unhappy self-deluding man has bitten *himself* fast. The Höidal mines in the bowels of the earth, where Gregers lived in seclusion for 17 years, suggest that underworld. Relling later explicitly makes the connection to Hades: "its a thousand pities [Gregers] didn't go to hell through one of the Höidal mines," he says (766. v. also 776: *Relling*. "May the devil fly away with you!" (McFarlane: "What a pity the man didn't get to hell out of it down one of those mines at Höidal." And for "May the devil fly away with you!" "God damn you!")

We find similar allusions in *An Enemy of the People*. Stockmann, too, thinks himself one whose mission is to reveal the Truth to others. As we have observed, self-deception also transforms that supreme egotist, who compares himself to Christ, into an agent of the Father of Lies. (There, too, we find soot associated with the infernal regions: "—what's her name—devil take it, the girl who has always got soot on her nose—"[277].)

Gregers' exalted conception of Hjalmar is clearly without foundation. That should be as evident to him as it is to Relling and to the audience. To cite but one reason: he was present when Hjalmar pretended not to recognize old Ekdal and in fact criticized Hjalmar for it. He believes in this illusion chiefly because it permits him to regard his father as a destructive monster who has "compassed about with all this treachery" the "extraordinary" Hjalmar "with his great, confiding, childlike mind" (717). The hatred that actually drives Gregers thus metamorphosis into the more acceptable emotion of compassion for a wronged innocent. He too has defective vision, perceiving only what he would perceive.

Hjalmar is no better. The disjunction between the man he thinks he is and is in fact is virtually complete. He believes himself a "breadwinner" who sacrifices all for his family, whose "invention"—really an excuse for after-dinner naps—will redeem them. He is in fact self-absorbed, self-pitying, lazy, extravagant, and indifferent to the financial well being of his family and to the sacrifices wife and daughter make to maintain his grandiose illusions. We can readily perceive how one so self-indulgent and so adept at self-deception could have convinced himself years ago of Werle's philanthropic benevolence if his creature-comforts depended upon it.

Gregers enters while Hjalmar and Ekdal are at work in their "forest." He tells Hedvig, who is alone, not to disturb them. He has failed in his attempt to liberate old Ekdal from his illusions and so turns his attention to the girl.

As noted, the wild duck represents for Gregers all that is false in the Ekdal's situation, in particular their dependence upon his despised father to whom they owe the duck. He attempts to make Hedvig conscious of the relationship between the duck dying in submarine darkness and her captive household. Hedvig's response indicates that she has already begun to perceive it:

> *Hedvig.* … And then there is so much that is strange about the wild duck. Nobody knows her, and nobody knows where she came from either.
>
> *Gregers.* And she has been down in the depths of the sea.
>
> *Hedvig.* … Why do you say "depths of the sea." … It sounds so strange to me when other people speak of the depths of the sea … [for] whenever I come to realize suddenly—in a flash—what is in there, it always seems to me that the whole room and everything in it should be called "the depths of the sea." —But that is so stupid.
>
> *Gregers.* You mustn't say that.
>
> *Hedvig.* Oh, yes, for you know it is only a garret.
>
> *Gregers* (*looks fixedly at her*). Are you so sure of that?
>
> *Hedvig* (*astonished*). That it is a garret?
>
> *Gregers.* Are you quite certain of it? (750–751)

The garret provides Hedvig with a fantasy world that rectifies or "retouches" the shortcomings of reality much as it does for old Ekdal. It affords the illusion of freedom in a "woodland" she cannot otherwise visit. It is the habitat of her beloved duck, with whom she shares so much. There she has found marvelous books left behind by "an old sea captain" called "The Flying Dutchman." She cannot read the books, which are in English. But the illustrations enable her to travel in imagination to foreign lands. Her "intuition" that the garret is "undersea" reflects her dawning understanding that she has but substituted one prison for another. Gregers wishes to encourage this realization and so asks "don't you wish you could travel and see the real world for yourself"? But Hedvig replies "I mean always to stay at home and help father and mother" (750). Her remark suggests that this adolescent is beginning to sense what the family's constant concern for her failing vision intimates: she is going blind and will not be able to leave her make-believe world.

Wagner's Flying Dutchman—to whom Ibsen probably refers—is redeemed from the sea by a woman who sacrifices herself for him. At the conclusion of the opera the two ascend heavenward towards the Eternal Light symbolic, for Ibsen, of truth. Ibsen's "Flying Dutchman" drowns in the lightless depths symbolic of self-deceit. Hedvig's fate bears a certain likeness: she will "drown" in the simulated forest which she regards as undersea, another victim of untruth. Both share the fate of the wild duck absent salvation from the deep by a "clever dog." The girl's tragedy—and the captain's—is anticipated by an engraving of "Death with an hour-glass" that illustrates the frontispiece of one of the captain's volumes (749). His many books indicate that this sea-dweller also found solace in illusion via the very books that now serve that function for Hedvig in her submarine world. Hedvig "should love above everything else to engrave pictures like those in the English books." Ibsen suggests that his "Flying Dutchman," who possessed a "paint box," hoped, like her, to find in artistic "retouching" refuge from a difficult reality (749).

Hedvig's sacrificial death does not, as in Wagner, liberate the living-dead, but, as in the captain's case, leads to "death by water." As Relling later notes, the Ekdals, after the tragedy that momentarily enlightens them, will return to their undersea prison; will "drown" like Ibsen's Dutchman. Gregers, who has learned nothing, will remain in his subterranean hell.

When shown the duck in daylight Gregers emphasizes the injury caused by Werle's "slugs"—the broken wing and crippled foot (753). He wants to make the Ekdals conscious of the hurt Werle has done them. Soon after he says to Hjalmar:

> My dear Hjalmar, I almost think you have something of the wild duck in you. You have dived down and bitten yourself fast in the undergrowth ... you have strayed into a poisonous marsh, Hjalmar; an insidious disease has taken hold of you, and you have sunk down to die in the dark (757).

Hjalmar rebuffs him, but Gregers persists:

Relling (to Gregers).	Come now, don't you find it pleasant, for once in a way, to sit at a well-spread table in a happy family circle?
Hjalmar.	Ah, yes, I really prize these social hours.
Gregers.	For my part, I don't thrive in marsh vapors.
Relling.	Marsh vapors?
Hjalmar.	Oh, don't begin with that stuff again
Gina.	Goodness knows there's no vapors in this house, Mr. Werle. I give the place a good airing every blessed day.
Gregers (leaves the table).	No airing you can give will drive out the taint I mean.
Hjalmar.	Taint! ...
Relling.	Excuse me—may it not be you yourself that have brought the taint from those mines up there? (762)

Hedvig is at table and overhears this exchange. The phrase "marsh vapors" is directed at her as well as to Hjalmar and Relling. She has already indicated she is sensitive to its implications.

In the competition for possession of Hjalmar's soul, Relling appears to figure as inferior advocate and defender of the life-lie, and Gregers as superior advocate for the Truth. But, as noted, the "truth" is Gregers' hatred of his father, not his concern for Hjalmar. Gregers believes in the fiction that the Ideal drives him, just as Hjalmar believes in the fiction that he is the breadwinner who sacrifices all for his family. Truth does not exist in Ibsen's cosmos, which, if ruled at all, is ruled not by a benevolent God but, as noted, by the Father of Lies, Prince of Darkness or Untruth, Progenitor of self-deception and illusion. Gregers is but one blind man among many. Relling, too, is blind to the fictions in which he believes; but he does at least clearly perceive others' blindness:

Gregers.	I should hardly have thought that I was quite stone blind.
Relling.	Yes you are—or not far from it. (795)

The act ends with Gregers asking Hjalmar to take "a long walk." He fears the countervailing influence of his adversary, Relling. Moreover, he has just had an unsatisfying encounter with his father which has revived ancient hatreds that require the "enlightenment" of Hjalmar, who must be made to realize precisely how odious Werle is. Werle is well aware that Gregers real, if unspoken, agenda, is motivated by hatred of him:

> *Werle.* From something you let fall last evening, and from your coming to lodge with the Ekdals, I can't help inferring that you intend to make yourself unpleasant to me in one way or another.

Gregers responds with his usual excuse. He exists to serve Truth. His "mission" just happens to coincide with making himself "unpleasant" to his father:

> *Gregers.* I intend to open Hjalmar Ekdal's eyes. He shall see his position as it really is—that is all. … The wrong done to old Ekdal, both by me and by—others can never be undone; but Hjalmar I can rescue from all the falsehood and deception that are bringing him to ruin." (764)

Gregers renounces the inheritance legally his upon his father's marriage in part because old Ekdal's freedom was its price. That impulse, and the constant, profound hatred of his father it implies, was evident early on. At Höidal Gregers accepted only the salary of a common workman. He strove to be independent of Werle, to detach himself from one whom he both loathed and feared.

Nonetheless, he remained in his father's employ. His hypocritical dependency, and the self-loathing it occasioned, also account for his renunciation of his inheritance. He insists that Hjalmar make the sacrifice he did not at Höidal by rejecting Werle's deed of gift, which he regards as an attempt by Werle to purchase "absolution" for his many sins and therefore tainted. The gift would insure the family's welfare and Hedvig's future—a matter of some importance given that she will eventually become blind, as Gregers well knows from conversation with Hjalmar (730). Gregers condemned his father for allowing the Ekdals to "go to the wall." But the criticism is apparently now forgotten; for he would insure that they are utterly and permanently destitute. Hatred of his father leads him to think this preferable to their continued dependence upon Werle. He, not Werle, or for that matter Relling, is to determine the Ekdals' future.

Act IV

Gregers' "long walk" with Hjalmar has the desired effect. Hjalmar now despises Werle and is suspicious of Gina. His remarks when he returns reveal that Gregers has told him Gina had probably been Werle's mistress while in his employ; that his father was entrapped by Werle long ago; and that old

Ekdal has, in consequence, been receiving payments greater than mere copying would justify. All of this could have been known, or at least suspected, by Hjalmar previously had he not wished it out of existence.

As noted, Gregers accuses himself and "others" (namely Werle) for the wrong done old Ekdal. There is, however, no indication that this champion of Truth mentions his own cowardly failure to intervene to Hjalmar during their walk. His revelation of "Truth" is here, as elsewhere, singularly focused on the malevolence and malfeasance of his father.

Gina later reveals that Werle "had his way" with her only after the death of his wife, when she was no longer his housekeeper. Gregers' mother—convinced of an affair that did not then exist—was, therefore, probably the source of his accusation. But anxious as he was to destroy his father's reputation Gregers assumed suspicion to be truth, and transmitted it as such to Hjalmar.

Hjalmar, who was in his youth an imitator adept at citing the works of others, obligingly parrots Gregers' accusations. He has momentarily "absorbed" from that source a reluctance to be contaminated by anything Werle has touched, and the conviction that because of Werle's baleful machinations he is now entrapped in "a swamp of deceit." Self-delusion is, however, as active as ever. Indeed, he now suffers from the new delusion that he is no longer deluded:

> *Hjalmar.* And I, too, thought my home such a pleasant one. That was a delusion. Where shall I now find the elasticity of spirit to bring my invention into the world of reality? Perhaps it will die with me; and then it will be your past, Gina, that will have killed it. (774)

There is of course no invention. The entirety of Hjalmar's self-pitying, accusatory outburst is false. Ibsen has cleverly given him a sympathetic and devoted wife who is not terribly bright; a daughter intelligent and perceptive enough but brought up in relative isolation, who knows only what her deluded parent has instilled; and an alcoholic father who prefers illusion to reality. Others would have seen through Hjalmar's pretentious posturing long ago.

Gregers' does not; for he is as self-deceiving, as "blind" as Hjalmar and the others. How else are we to explain his exaltation of this egocentric mediocrity, and his expectation that the revelation of painful, destructive truths will lead to family harmony? For seventeen years he has nursed hatred, fear and envy of his father (764). Now, having successfully instilled in Hjalmar the same hatred, he ironically preaches forgiveness and reconciliation: "surely nothing in the world can compare with the joy of forgiving one who has erred" he tells him (775). The previously gloomy Gregers is able for the first time to rejoice.

He enters "*his face beaming with satisfaction*" *before* he has opportunity to see the effect of his disclosures on the Ekdals, satisfied that he has accomplished his real, if unstated and unconscious purpose (774).

Hatred of his father in one who advises forgiveness has not abated. He refuses to listen when Bertha and Gina speak favorably of Werle: "If you ladies are going to follow up on this topic, I had better withdraw," he says (780). He rejects Hjalmar's conclusion that Werle and Bertha "will realize the true marriage" based upon "mutual confession and absolution" (782). And in fact that is not the case—*cannot* be the case in Ibsen's cosmos. Bertha's account reveals that Werle has "sanitized" his past; and, as we have noted, she very likely plans to graze in other pastures once her husband becomes completely blind. The two have for the moment simply agreed to accept each other's fictions. But Gregers cannot reconcile himself to even the appearance of honest disclosure by the couple. Transparent, truthful family relationships interest him only when they lead to condemnation of his father, not when they benefit him. Werle must, in effect, cease to exist for the Ekdals.

Gregers intervenes immediately when Bertha offers Hjalmar financial help:

Bertha.	If there is anything Werle can do for you [Hjalmar], you must just apply to Graberg.
Gregers.	That offer I am sure Hjalmar Ekdal will decline with thanks." (781)

Urged on by Gregers, Hjalmar rejects the prospect of financial independence, although now virtually destitute. He proposes to repay Werle's past contributions to old Ekdal "with five per cent. interest" from the proceeds of his non-existent invention. For his own reasons Gregers chooses to believe Hjalmar's evasions and fantasies, and indeed encourages them:

Hjalmar.	There now Gregers; I have got that burden of debt off my mind.
Gregers.	You will soon, at all events.
Hjalmar.	I think my attitude may be called correct.
Gregers.	You are the man I have always taken you for. (782)

We subsequently learn that Werle has arranged for generous monthly payments to old Ekdal. After his death Hedvig is to continue to receive the payments for life. Gregers wants Hjalmar to reject Werle's deed of gift even if it results in utter impoverishment: He intervenes when the family is offered it saying it is a "trap" that will reveal the mercenary Hjalmar to *be* mercenary. He is blind to this obvious truth:

Gregers.	Hjalmar, this is a trap he is setting for you.
Hjalmar.	Do you think it's another trap?
Gregers.	When he was here this morning he said: Hjalmar Ekdal is not the man you imagine him to be.
Hjalmar.	Not the man—!
Gregers.	That you shall see, he said.
Hjalmar.	He meant you should see that I would allow myself to be bought off— …
Gregers.	Yes, Hilmar—now is the time to show who was right, he or I. (786)

But this is not what Werle said. In fact, as we have seen, by suppressing or ignoring inconvenient truths Hjalmar has repeatedly allowed himself "to be bought off." However, Werle does not explicitly accuse him of that. The actual exchange, which occurs before the Ekdals and Hjalmar learn of the deed of gift, reveals that Gregers converts Werle's tentative, questioning remarks—which have to do with the revelation of certain "truths" by Gregers and with money only by implication—into certainty:

Gregers.	… The wrong done to old Ekdal … can never be undone; but Hjalmar I can rescue from all the falsehood and deception that are bringing him to ruin.
Werle.	Do you think that will be doing him a kindness?
Gregers.	I have not the least doubt of it.
Werle.	You think our worthy photographer is the sort of man to appreciate such friendly offices?
Gregers.	Yes, I do.
Werle.	H'm—we shall see. (764)

Hjalmar's reaction to Gregers' misrepresentation is characteristically false. He tears the deed of gift carefully and "lays both pieces on the table." The option then exists to later repair it and claim it for his father, his daughter, and himself, which he subsequently does. Meanwhile he pretends to be the principled idealist he is not.

Gregers enters immediately after Hjalmar repairs the document. Scissors, gum pot and brush are still on the table in plain view with the repaired deed of gift (805). Were it not for his momentary "blindness" Gregers would see those articles and deduce what has happened. However, should he see what is plainly before him, his idol, Hjalmar, would crumble, and the continued, pervasive influence of Werle would be confirmed. Therefore, he does not see.

We perceive from the preceding exchanges and from others like them that the intervention of the "idealistic" Gregers does not result in a genuine conflict between representatives of the "life-lie" and of truth, but rather in the deeper decent of both parties into illusion.

Although he suspects Hedvig's parentage, Gregers says nothing about it during his long walk with Hjalmar. Had he done so Hjalmar would have reacted violently as he later does when he concludes that Hedvig may not be his child. Gregers hopes to prevent that. When Mrs. Sörby remarks that Werle "is going blind," Gregers, fearing that Hjalmar might connect Werle's infirmity with Hedvig's, anxiously interjects: "Hush, don't speak of that here" (780). He actively suppresses what he regards as an inconvenient truth.

We have to wonder at this. If Gregers really put Truth before all, then he should have conveyed his suspicions to Hjalmar. If his primary purpose is to discredit Werle, disclosure would also be advantageous. His evident concern and affection for the young girl who may be his half sister perhaps restrains him. If his friendship with Hedvig is to eventually blossom into something more, it is essential he believe her dubious parentage allows for that possibility. Even if we exclude this motive, should it be established that Hedvig is actually Werle's child, Werle will have won: he will in effect have become a permanent presence in the Ekdal family.

Gina subsequently tells Hjalmar she does not know whether Hedvig is Werle's child or his. Hjalmar puts the worst possible construction on her ambiguous revelation in part because Hedvig and Werle are both losing their sight but also because it gives him the perfect opportunity to wallow in self-pity: "I have no child!" he cries. The egocentric blindness that has always plagued him—indeed plagues nearly all in this drama—becomes the leading motif. Gina cries "Look at the child, Ekdal. Look at the child!" "I will not," "I cannot! I must get out—away from all this!" he says—before storming out to drown his sorrows in drink (787). This blind man ironically rejects his daughter because of her incipient blindness.

Gregers is aware that Hedvig knows Werle is responsible for the gift of her beloved wild duck (736). As he wants Hjalmar to choose between him and Werle by renouncing Werle's deed of gift, so he wants Hedvig to choose between Werle's gift of the duck and her father, or, really, between Werle and Gregers who now advises her. She, too, must renounce Werle's gift and thus demonstrate her allegiance to Gregers. His cruel suggestion that Hedvig destroy what is dearest to her, a sacrifice which he admits might not have the desired effect ("try it" [790]), is in part a test of her affection for him. She must be beholden to Gregers not to Werle. That would surely be the case should the death of the duck restore the relationship between Hjalmar and Hedvig.

Hedvig is not to tell her mother. Gina, well aware of Hedvig's devotion to Hjalmar, suspicious of Gregers, and confident her husband will eventually come around, would of course prohibit it.

Act V

"Dr. Relling, I shall not give up the struggle until I have rescued Hjalmar from your clutches" says Gregers (797). And much of this act focuses upon the combat between the two. Hedvig, the one person really committed to the truth as she perceives it, and for whom subterfuge or dissembling are impossible, is the unfortunate casualty. Relling contributes to her death by encouraging the Ekdals' illusions in which the duck plays a central role; Gregers by insisting that Hedvig destroy the duck and with it those illusions. For the physician Relling the life-lie is a "narcotic" that insures the well being of his "patients." It is anathema to Gregers notwithstanding the fact he lives such a lie. Relling accuses him of "integrity fever," and "hero worship" that blind him to Hjalmar's obvious faults (795). He diagnoses the symptoms accurately but omits the cause, which he cannot know. Both "integrity fever" and "hero worship" are owing to Gregers' hatred of his father, whom he regards as dishonest, malevolent, and the very antithesis of a "hero." They are components of the hatred motivating him throughout, even to hatred of self because descended from and dependent upon Werle.

Soon after Relling expounds his theory of the life-lie to Gregers, he presents him with two instances, saying to Hedvig "Well, little wild-duck-mother, I'm just going down to see whether papa is still meditating upon that wonderful invention of his" (797). His casual remark convinces Gregers of the need to rescue Hedvig—who wisely has had second thoughts about sacrificing her beloved duck—from the doctor's clutches, now manifest to Gregers as the "life-lies" promulgated by Relling. And so he again insists that Hedvig destroy the bird in order to regain her father's love. By acting as he advises, she is to demonstrate her commitment to Gregers rather than to Relling, as before she was to prefer Gregers to Werle. Gregers is obviously aware of Hedvig's profound, selfless commitment to Hjalmar. Were she not completely devoted she would never consider killing her beloved pet. For selfish reasons which he almost certainly does not appreciate, and because he is blind to Hjalmar's limitations, Gregers asks for a sacrifice based upon a proposition a moment's reflection would reveal as absurd—namely, that Hedvig has insufficiently demonstrated her love for her father.

The naïve Hedvig seriously considers Gregers' advice. Her decision to actually kill the bird is triggered by the arrival of Hjalmar who believes, or pretends to believe, Hedvig no longer loves him. This blind man clings to his blindness, refusing to even look at the daughter, who, blind to his faults, blindly loves him, ordering her out of his sight when their paths cross. Those actions coupled with Gregers' "advice"—rooted not in his love for Truth or the Ideal, but in his hatred of his father, his struggle with Relling, his absurd elevation of Hjalmar, and hence also manifestations of blindness—are sufficient to determine her:

> *Hedvig (stands a moment immovable, in terror and perplexity, biting her lips to keep back the tears; then she clenches her hands convulsively and says softly).* The wild duck. *[She steals over and takes the pistol from the shelf, opens the garret door a little ways, creeps in and draws the door to after her.* (801–802)

In fact Hjalmar does not plan to abandon his family or his daughter. As Gina correctly perceives, he values the comforts of domesticity far too much. He would have remained if only to gain access to Ekdal's and Hedvig's inheritance. We have a clear indication of this, and of his intent to remain, when he reassembles the torn deed of gift, which Hedvig has promised to bestow upon him when it passes to her. In the meantime Gina will as before be the custodian of old Ekdal's substantial income. Hjalmar knows he will benefit just as he did in the past.

But the innocent girl believes that Hjalmar's dishonest posturing truly represents his beliefs. She is convinced by Gregers, blind to Hjalmar's faults, that her father will never again accept her, love her, or remain with the family unless she kills the duck.

We soon hear its quack. Hedvig has disturbed it by placing the gun against its breast. But she cannot kill her beloved pet. Through the thin partitions that enclose the garret she hears Hjalmar, the most selfish of men, accuse her of selfishness. (Moi notes that Ibsen allows us to hear the quack of the duck to indicate that the voices of Hjalmar and Gregers are audible to Hedvig.)[22] Hjalmar—who has publicly and ostentatiously "renounced" his interest in the deed of gift—is concerned lest he be deprived of the income. He "retouches" this selfish, demeaning impulse. Avarice metamorphoses into fear that the girl, who unhesitatingly offered up her share of her inheritance to her father, will abandon him and take her gift with her. Illusion once more replaces truth. The innocent becomes the guilty; the guilty becomes the innocent betrayed:

Hjalmar. If … others came with the glamour of wealth about them [McFarlane: "their hands full"] and called to the child:—"Leave him: come to us: here life awaits you—! [McFarlane: "life is at your feet"] … If I then asked her: Hedvig, are you willing to renounce that life [McFarlane: "this life"] for me? (*Laughs scornfully*) No thank you! You would soon hear what answer I would get." [A *pistol shot is heard from within the garret.* (808)

In view of the pervasive influence of illusion and self-deception in this drama, it is possible that the girl misunderstands Hjalmar's remark to mean "Hedvig, are you willing to renounce *existence* for me?" If that is true we can perhaps conclude that she mistakenly and unnecessarily offers her death as proof of her devotion. If not true, then she perhaps erroneously believes she faces a lifetime of hostile rejection by the person whom she loves above all, and so shoots herself. In either case her death becomes one more error in this tragic comedy of errors. She assumes that what is unreal is real just as her elders do.

There is another possibility. Ibsen specifies a two-barreled pistol. One barrel has been discharged; one is still loaded. Hedvig perhaps intends to kill the duck when she enters the fictive forest. Terrified and perplexed by her father's rejection, she says "The wild duck" immediately before taking the pistol from the shelf and stealing into the garret. (802). She attempts to shoot the bird—and by pressing the weapon against its breast elicits the "quack" which we hear—but triggers the empty barrel. Unfamiliar with the weapon, in the dim light of the garret, she accidentally shoots herself by discharging the loaded barrel while attempting to find out why the gun has misfired. The powder burns that Relling notices simply indicate that Hedvig was holding the weapon close to her breast at the time, which we might expect of one with failing vision. What she thinks innocuous is in fact deadly—precisely the error of all in the Ekdal household. If that was what actually happened, then the Ekdals and their associates mourn for the wrong reason. The truth remains permanently inaccessible to those committed to the life-lie.

Relling despises Gregers and is at war with him. He had warned the Ekdals of their lodger's pernicious influence, in particular of the danger to Hedvig (776–777). He naturally prefers, and so delivers, a verdict of suicide—which implicates his enemy and confirms his "diagnosis" of Gregers' "illness"—to that of accidental death. (Relling: "No one shall ever convince me that the pistol went off by accident" [812].) His conclusion is arguably proof of his own blindness. We need not accept it. If Hedvig's death was accidental, she is not "one human being capable of the supreme idealistic gesture of self-sacrifice," as Brian Johnston argues,[23] but another, and the most tragic, victim of the illusions that afflict all in this drama.

The gun is the very weapon with which old Ekdal and Hjalmar pretended suicide (755–756), and with which the deluded old man killed his fictive bears, which were actually rabbits. Hedvig's hand remains tightly clasped around it in death. She will be buried clutching it. Ibsen insisted that the pistol remain visible as Hedvig is carried offstage,[24] and rightly so; for it symbolizes the motif that penetrates and unifies the drama, and in fact precedes it—as noted, it informs the illegality that brought about old Ekdal's downfall—namely, the deadly effects of pretense, illusion, falsification or "retouching" when taken for fact. As Old Ekdal remarks a second time, accurately summarizing the dreadful sequence of events, "The woods avenge themselves." (810)

Gregers omits any mention of his own contribution to this disaster during an earlier conversation with Hjalmar in which he implies that Hedvig will, or has, killed the duck (808). He leaves the impression that it was entirely Hedvig's idea, which she has secretly conveyed to him:

Hjalmar.	… I cannot shake off this frightful doubt—perhaps Hedvig has never really and honestly loved me.
Gregers.	What would you say if she were to give you a proof of her love. (*Listens*). What's that? I thought I heard the wild duck—
Hjalmar.	It's the wild duck quacking. Father's in the attic.
Gregers.	Is he? (*His face lights up with joy*). I say, you may have the proof that your poor misunderstood Hedvig loves you! (806–807)
	…………………………………………………………………
Gina (*comes in*).	Oh, Ekdal, I can hear grandfather blazing away in the garret by hisself.
Hjalmar.	I'll look in.
Gregers (*eagerly, with emotion*).	Wait a moment! Do you know what that was?
Hjalmar.	Yes, of course I know.
Gregers.	No, you don't know. But *I* do. That was the proof!
Hjalmar.	What proof?
Gregers.	It was a child's free-will offering. She has got your father to shoot the wild duck. … She wanted to sacrifice to you her most cherished possession; for then she thought you would surely come to love her again. (808)

Gregers' reaction immediately after hearing the shot is noteworthy. He says *quietly*; "I knew it; I knew the child would make amends." (McFarlane: "I knew … that redemption would come through the child.") Besotted as he is with his false "idol," Hjalmar, and with pursuit of those "Truths" that obscure his actual motives, he puts the entire burden of reconciliation on the innocent child who dreaded the rupture with her father. His remark confirms the false impression that the "sacrifice" of her beloved duck was Hedvig's unprompted, self-willed action.

After he learns of Hedvig's death Gregers becomes almost silent. He advised, indeed insisted, that she shoot the duck, and so shares responsibility with Hjalmar for her death, if it was in fact suicide. If her death was accidental, he is completely responsible. And those are facts that this Knight who serves Truth, and requires uncompromising truthfulness from others, prefers to conceal. He can conceal it; for no one overheard his conversations with Hedvig:

Relling (goes over to Gregers *and says).*	No one shall ever convince me that the pistol went off by accident.
Gregers (who has stood terrified with convulsive twitchings).	Who can say how the dreadful thing happened? (812)

Those are Gregers only comments touching upon his central, critical role in Hedvig's death. He follows it immediately with the sanctimonious rubbish that has shielded him throughout. It enables him to look upon his deadly interference as productive rather than destructive. One clearly perceives how he, like Hjalmar, transforms or "retouches" reality to suit himself; and how he uses his friend to conceal his own reprehensible actions, as before he used him to conceal, from himself and from others, the hatred of Werle that actually drove him:

Gregers.	Hedvig has not died in vain. Did you not see how sorrow set free what is noble in [Hjalmar]? ... Why should [this induced nobility] not endure and increase throughout his life? (812)

As in many of Ibsen's plays inheritance is crucial. One inevitably inherits what Ibsen regards as universal moral failings. "The sins of the fathers are visited on the children." The renunciation of his inheritance by Gregers, and of the Ekdal's "inheritance" or deed of gift by Hjalmar are profoundly ironic; for strictly speaking renunciation of one's inheritance is impossible in Ibsen's cosmos.

If we compare the Werle and Ekdal families we notice a striking difference. Both Werles are very sure of themselves. Gregers is as sure that his father ruined the life of his mother as Werle is that she was simply an "overstrained" alcoholic (711–712) whose religious beliefs resulted in endless, insufferable "penitential sermons" (780). Both are quite willing to do whatever is necessary to achieve their ends. Both are convinced the Ekdals have sunk down to die in darkness. Both believe they have the right to interfere in the lives of others. Werle ruined old Ekdal, passed on his woman and perhaps his illegitimate offspring to the son, and provided the Ekdals with a new life as photographers. Gregers sought to undo what his detested father had done and so, intervening again, changed the Ekdals' life decisively and irrevocably. The similarity of son to father indicates that Greger's egocentric self-deception and blindness were inherited. Gregers' attempt to distinguish himself from his father was always doomed. He may be Werle's inferior but he is not his antithesis. His conviction that he is, is but an illusion that, like his elevation and transformation of Hjalmar, confirms his inheritance of his father's imperfect "vision," defined as reluctance or inability to perceive painful, condemnatory truths.

The Ekdals are by contrast passive and submissive, as they must be if the Werles are to work their wills upon them. Hjalmar was known in his youth for citing the works of others. He was in effect a dependent, a follower. Photography is an apt profession for such; for the unretouched photo is but a copy of reality. He inherited those traits from his father, "always an ass" according to Relling, a weak man, a follower also, and so as easily misled by Werle as Hjalmar is by Gregers. His occupation of copyist is similar in significance to his son's and equally appropriate. There is no indication that old Ekdal fought the charges brought against him, although they may have been unjust. The circumstances of his trial are unknown to us, but we do know that neither father nor son protested or now protests them. Like the wild duck the Ekdals have accommodated, becoming dependents of the man who "wounded" them. And that dependency will continue in future notwithstanding Gregers' intervention and Hjalmar's "new" understanding of Werle's nefarious actions.

The single characteristic which the Werle's share with the Ekdals is blindness, the inability to "see" or to acknowledge what one does not wish to. This trait, inherited from our first parents, is shared by nearly all of Ibsen's protagonists.

Hedvig's death is the result of a confluence of such "familial" traits. They are her inheritance as surely as the deed of gift. Her death on the day of her birth suggests the infirmity passed on from parent to child at the moment of birth. Her incipient physical blindness affirms the intellectual and moral blindness inherited from both families. She derived from Werle, from old Ekdal and from Hjalmar the inability to distinguish truth from fiction. Like the wild duck, with which she identifies, she confuses light and darkness, death and life, underworld and upper world, clinging to what is death-dealing in the mistaken belief that it is life-bestowing. (Her misadventure with the pistol, if genuine, would signify precisely this.) She cannot see Hjalmar's ridiculous posturings for what they are. Nor for that matter can he. He has inherited his blindness, his immersion in illusion, from his father. But for that to end in Hedvig's death Gregers' intervention is required, and the inherited blindness that induces her to follow his deadly advice—the result of *his* inherited blindness—which he falsely presents as "that which gives life its value" (797).

Gregers is blind to the fact that his actual end is the defeat of Werle; blind to the possible consequences of his interference for Hedvig, Gina and Hjalmar; blind to the shortcomings of his "hero" Hjalmar; blind to the ridiculous notion that the disclosure of painful truths will automatically result in ideal marriage. In this respect, he resembles the girl who may be his half sister. As in Hedda, the past overshadows the present; and the results are equally disastrous. To cite again what Hedvig says of the wild duck: "And then there is so much that is strange about the wild duck. Nobody knows her, and nobody knows where she came from either." (750–751)

The girl of course unwittingly describes herself. Her paternity is doubtful, and her innocent commitment to illusion is exceptional or "strange." As we have observed the wild duck represents all in this drama. Hence, Hedvig's words also describe the "strange" preference of fallen, exiled humankind for illusion, and its fatal consequences. Ibsen's protagonists move in impenetrable darkness created by their past, remote as well as recent, and by that preference—darkness that isolates one from another and indeed oneself from oneself. They do not know themselves; nobody knows them; and they know nobody.

Thirteen has long been an "unlucky" number. The elder Werle regards it as such (700). Gregers final characterization of himself as the "thirteenth at table" suggests that he has not abandoned his crusade to discredit his father. He intends, in future, to further disclose and advertise Werle's wrongs. In Christian symbolism "Thirteen is the number of faithlessness and betrayal. At the Last Supper there were thirteen persons at the table: Jesus and the twelve Apostles, including Judas, who had already agreed to betray his master."[25] It is possible that this son of a religious mother, convinced that he is committed to Truth and to the Ideal, identifies with the followers of Christ. As we have observed the commitment is, in Gregers' case, a life-lie that enables him to pursue his real, if unconscious, agenda. Given the tragic events for which he is responsible, the thirteenth man Gregers actually, if perhaps unwittingly, resembles is Judas, another agent of the Father of Lies and betrayer of the son of man. *That* "thirteenth at table" is largely responsible for the death of Hedvig. Relling's parting observation is quite accurate

Relling.	May I inquire what is your destiny?
Gregers (going).	To be the thirteenth at table.
Relling.	The devil it is. (813)[26]

Notes

1. Arnold Bennet in McFarlane, *Henrik Ibsen: A Critical Anthology*, 188.
2. Hermann J. Weigand, *Modern Ibsen*, 164.
3. Hermann J. Weigand, *Modern Ibsen*, 163.
4. Richard Hornby, *Patterns*, 48.
5. T. R. Henn in McFarlane, *Henrik Ibsen: A Critical Anthology*, 207.
6. Toril Moi, "It was as if." 670.
7. James McFarlane in *Henrik Ibsen: An Enemy of the People, The Wild Duck, Rosmerholm*, xvii.
8. John Northam, *Critical Study*, 144. For a more extensive review of critical opinion see Machiraju, A. F., "Ideals and Victims, "134–142.
9. Hermann J. Weigand, *Modern Ibsen*, 135.
10. James McFarlane, *Henrik Ibsen: A Critical Anthology*, 245.
11. James McFarlane, *Henrik Ibsen: A Critical Anthology*, 104.
12. James McFarlane, *Henrik Ibsen: A Critical Anthology*, 273.
13. Maryam Beyad, "Ibsen's *The Wild Duck*," 8.
14. John Northam, *Critical Study*, 113.
15. John Northam, *Critical Study*, 117.
16. Charles R. Lyons, *Divided Consciousness*, 93.
17. Robert Raphael in Fjelde, *Critical Essays*, 121.
18. John Northam, *Critical Study*, 114.
19. Henrik Ibsen, in Moi, "It was as if …," 674.
20. John Northam, *Critical Study*, 117.
21. Toril Moi, "It was as if …," 663.
22. Toril Moi, "It was as if …," 685 fn. 31.
23. Brian Johnston in Lyons, *Divided Consciousness*, 96.
24. Henrik Ibsen in McFarlane, *Henrik Ibsen: A Critical Anthology*, 104.
25. George Ferguson, *Signs and Symbols*, 154.
26. "Afan trod et," "The devil believe it" (Moi, "It was as if …," 681).

References

All parenthetical page citations in this text are from *Eleven Plays of Henrik Ibsen*, ed. B. A. Cerf, D. S. Klopfer. New York: *The Modern Library*, 1935. Translators not given but those of plays discussed in this volume appear to be R. Farquharson Sharp (*Ghosts*, *An Enemy of the People*), Edmund Gosse and William Archer (*The Master Builder*, *Hedda Gabler*), and William Archer (*The Wild Duck*). I found those older translations satisfactory for my purposes. In the few cases where translation appeared to be an issue I have appended parallel citations from *The Oxford Ibsen* (McFarlane, James Walter, ed. and trans. *The Oxford Ibsen*, 8 vols. London: Oxford University Press, 1962).

Beyad, Maryam, and Mahsa Moradpour. "Ibsen's *The Wild Duck* and Chekhov's *The Seagull*: Classical Tragedy in Modern Perspectives." *Pazhuhesh-e Zabanha-ye Khareji* 49, Special Issue, English (Winter 2009): 5–22.

Ferguson, George, ed. *Signs and Symbols in Christian Art*. Hesperides Book. New York: Oxford University Press, 1961.

Fjelde, Rolf, ed. *Ibsen: A Collection of Critical Essays*. Englewood Cliffs, NJ: Prentice-Hall, 1965.

Hornby, Richard. *Patterns in Ibsen's Middle Plays*. Lewisburg: Bucknell University Press, 1981.

Lyons, Charles R. *Henrik Ibsen: The Divided Consciousness*. Carbondale, IL: Southern Illinois University Press, 1972.

Machiraju, A. F. "Ideals and Victims: Ibsen's Concerns in *Ghosts* and *The Wild Duck*." *Modern Language Review* 87, no. 1 (January 1992): 134–142.

McFarlane, James, ed. *Henrik Ibsen: A Critical Anthology*. Harmondsworth, Middlesex, England: Penguin Books, 1970.

McFarlane, James, trans. *Henrik Ibsen: An Enemy of the People*, *The Wild Duck*, *Rosmerholm*. *Oxford World's Classics*. Oxford, England: Oxford University Press, 1999.

Moi, Toril. "'It was as if he meant something different from what he said—all the time': Language, Metaphysics and the Everyday in *The Wild Duck*." *New Literary History* 33, no. 4 (Autumn 2002): 655–686.

Northam, John. *Ibsen: A Critical Study*. Cambridge: Cambridge University Press, 1973.

Weigand, Hermann J. *The Modern Ibsen*. New York: Henry Holt & Co., 1925.

· 4 ·

HEDDA'S REVENGE

For Weigand "what characterizes Hedda more than anything else is a complete dearth of inner resources. Hers is a barren nature on which no seed has been able to thrive."[1] For Northam Hedda "dies for the vision of human potentiality superior to the reality to which life condemns her." She demonstrates "what it means to have heroic aspirations in an age that almost, but not quite, denies all possibility of heroism."[2] For McFarlane "Hedda Gabler is most convincingly read as the record of a series of personal campaigns for control and domination: over oneself, over others, and over one's world."[3] For Caroline W. Mayerson Hedda's "colossal egotism, her lack of self-knowledge, her cowardice, render her search for fulfillment but a succession of futile blunders which culminate in the supreme futility of death."[4] For Stein Haugum Olson "The cause of Hedda's tragedy is that her values are all aesthetic values. … The action of *Hedda Gabler* unfolds the disintegration of this aesthetic personality in its inevitable collision with the real world of action and moral choice."[5] Arthur Ganz, who perceives similarities between Nora and Hedda observes that "Both works are finally about a transcendent quest for the self, about creatures hemmed in by social circumstance and the limits of their own natures who yet are committed absolutely to a vision of fulfillment—of a self fully known, fully gratified, unimpeded by the bounds of common reality."[6]

None of these assessments sufficiently emphasizes the central issue, suggested by Ibsen in his preliminary notes:

> "She wants to lead a man's life. But then come hesitations—the inherited deep-rooted beliefs. ... One marries Tesman but one occupies one's imagination with Lövborg. One leans back in one's chair, closes one's eyes and pictures his adventures ... She cannot do it herself—cannot take part in the other one's goal—so she shoots herself."[7]

This brief description of thwarted desire developed at length into a tale of a soul at war with itself. In Hedda, the impulse to be free, to "live," which Ibsen associates with her wish "to lead a man's life" and enjoy the male's sexual freedom, is in constant conflict with "inherited deep rooted beliefs," in particular the culturally transmitted and implanted fear of what others will think or say should one exercise that freedom,

The conflict between the desire for freedom and self-imposed restraint is common enough, probably existing in all individuals at all times in some form to some degree. Hedda's internal conflict is, however, extreme, leading to impulsive, erratic, contradictory, vindictive and, ultimately, self-destructive behavior. Her fear of scandal is characteristic of the "proper" or "respectable" Hedda. Her fascination with forbidden, "illicit" sexuality is characteristic of the "other" passionate Hedda who resents the constraints society imposes upon the female as well as those imposed by the proper Hedda. The passionate Hedda condemns and rejects the fear of offending as unworthy. The proper Hedda fears the impulses of the passionate and allows them only surreptitious, oblique expression. Hedda's behavior in its entirety can be traced to this inner discord and the self-disgust it occasions.

The young Hedda avidly solicited accounts of Lövborg's "days and night of devilment" (554), which surely included sexual adventures in the company of women such as Mademoiselle Diana. The mature Hedda exhibits the same interest in illicit behavior. She willingly engages in verbal "foreplay" with Brack and would, if she could, be an invisible spectator at his parties (562), which she obviously associates with orgiastic abandonment—for it is there that she imagines Lövborg in the role of Dionysius, "with vine leaves in his hair." Yet she presents herself, and thinks of herself, as the very embodiment of propriety. Appearance and reality, head and heart, mind and body are in conflict. Hedda appears to be the paragon of self-control (Ibsen notes that "*Her steel-grey eyes express a cold, unruffled repose*"), but she cannot control rebellious, destructive impulses always seething below the surface. They become manifest as soon as Hedda is alone: "[*In the meantime Hedda walks about the room raising her arms and clutching her hands as if in desperation.* …]" (513–514).

The proper Hedda and the passionate are not in communication. Like the other protagonists we have considered, she does not know herself. Hedda's proper self refuses to consciously acknowledge the potency and immediacy of her "other" self's forbidden desires. They become manifest as an irrepressible wish to experience the sexual acts of others vicariously "in roundabout terms" (554), and as impulsive, destructive actions that circumvent consciousness and conscious control. Hedda envies the young Thea's beautiful hair. But to consciously concede envy would be to confirm possession by the "base" desire to make ones self sexually attractive. And that her proper self prohibits. Those suppressed, unacceptable impulses lead to self condemnation. Self condemnation is equally unacceptable and so also denied conscious expression. It metamorphoses into hatred of the object that elicits the forbidden emotions and desires and with it the impulse to destroy that object. In this instance it surfaces as a threat to burn off the young Thea's hair. Hedda herself is unaware of the source of this destructive urge and others like it. As she tells Brack: "these impulses come over me all of a sudden; and I cannot resist them … I don't know how to explain it" (541–542). Her divided, discordant nature prohibits self knowledge. Any interpretation which represents her as motivated by a "vision of human potentiality" or "transcendent quest for the self" is therefore untenable.

Hedda's divided nature determines in part the personae with which Ibsen surrounds her and aspects of the setting. The contrast between the dimly lit, curtained, windowless inner room with its portrait, and the well-lit "*spacious, handsome, and tastefully furnished drawing room*" suggests the contrast between the hidden and the overt Hedda. For the proper Hedda Ibsen has provided Tesman, for the passionate Lövborg. As Stein Haugom Olson notes "Lövborg is in every respect Tesman's opposite. Tesman is fair, Lövborg dark; Tesman is plump, Lövborg lean. Tesman is relatively poor with only his modest, inconsequential aunts, living on their annuity, to support him; Lövborg has inherited a considerable sum of money which he wastes, and has important influential relatives. Tesman is conventional; Lövborg consumes his life in debauchery and dissipation. Tesman collects, arranges, and interprets single details and objects; Lövborg synthesizes and attempts to reveal the grand design in the history of culture."[8] Each man bears a package symbolic of his significance. Tesman carries the worn slippers emblematic of his bourgeois domesticity and attachment to the past. Lövborg carries the revolutionary manuscript that challenges and redefines conventional thinking about the future. The two men are associated with contrasting women—Aunt Julia and Mademoiselle Diana—who express their very different personalities. They also reflect the conflict within Hedda between conformity and the desire for sexual freedom.

We perceive in Tesman, Lövborg, Thea and Brack similar if less extreme inner divisions. The naive, respectable Tesman clearly wishes to avoid returning Lövborg's lost manuscript—which will make his reputation at the expense of Tesman's—and defers it as long as possible. He deliberately offers this reformed alcoholic a drink pretending it is for Thea, who has not yet arrived (553); were Lövborg to become his dissolute former self he would no longer pose a threat. He deserts his wife for Thea seemingly without a qualm. As we shall note, he is motivated by the possibility of a future intimate relationship with Thea as well as by the scholarly impulse to reconstruct Lövborg's manuscript. Lövborg is capable of orgiastic abandonment as well as extraordinary intellectual achievements which require self-restraint. Respectable, rational, "judgmental" Brack repeatedly attempts to seduce the married Hedda and sponsors sybaritic parties. Compelled by her devotion to Lövborg, the conventional, submissive Thea defies social convention and leaves her husband. In all such cases the darker, passionate, "criminal" or irresponsible side acts independently of the rational, denying the individual complete knowledge of self.

Hedda's extraordinary behavior is chiefly the result of her upbringing by her father, the General. Probably a stern, authoritarian figure, given his occupation, he apparently wished for a boy child and so raised Hedda as such, teaching her to shoot for example. Yet he also thought of her as a vulnerable female. The General invariably "chaperoned" Hedda. He sat in the same room, ostensibly reading the newspaper, during her whispered, intimate conversations with Lövborg. Her introduction to the sexual and illicit occurred within earshot of the individual who attended her precisely to prevent this. One could never be sure that the General overheard nothing. Guilt and self-condemnation for soliciting forbidden topics and entertaining forbidden feelings were the consequences of those moments when the young Hedda "lived" most intensely. Displaced, that guilt and those feelings, still active in the adult, give rise to destructive impulses. The pistols inherited from her father symbolize the deadly continuing influence of parent upon child, of past upon present. They suggest both fascination with the phallus and the impulse to annihilate its bearer, or more broadly the conflict between the passionate and proper Hedda.

Her upbringing as a quasi-male imposed upon her a secondary, discordant masculine nature—evident, for example in her dislike of the scent of flowers (511, 543), her scornful rejection of the domesticity of Tesman and Julia, her marriage to the weak, effeminate Jörgen, and her utter lack of the pleasurable emotions associated with pregnancy—which intensified her longings for the sexual freedom and independence permitted only the male. As Ibsen wrote in the passage cited above, "She wants to lead a man's life." The conflict of licentiousness with prudishness, which qualifies virtually all of her actions, is chiefly the result of this divided male-female nature. Julia's description of the young Hedda riding out with the General, the masculine, phallic pistol almost certainly by her side, yet with "feminine" feathers adorning her hat (503), suggests a duality and inner tension between the illicit or masculine and the respectable or feminine of long standing. Her subsequent association with those polar opposites, the lascivious Brack and conservative Tesman reflects the same inner division.

As this example indicates, the young Hedda's history determines the mature Hedda's behavior. Her past defines—and confines—her. It determines beginning and end. Hedda first enters from the rear room with its portrait of the parent who "witnesses" all, and still in effect observes and controls her. Her suicide occurs there, hidden from the other protagonists, viewed only by the individual chiefly responsible for her inner conflicts. His portrait hangs over the sofa, and it is there, rather than at the piano or elsewhere, that Hedda shoots herself. As Evert Sprinchorn observes "Ibsen has divided upstage from downstage, inner room from living room, to suggest that the past is ever present in the lives of these people."[9]

Hers is the agony of one "Unable to fare forward or retreat." She can commit herself fully neither to the feminine nor to the masculine aspects of her character, neither to respectable conformity nor to Dionysian abandon, neither to mind nor to body. The "proper" Hedda, repelled by the physical intimacy it implies, cannot love. The sexual longings of the "other," sensual Hedda—who if liberated, would almost certainly be capable of love—are prohibited by her proper and conventional self. They cannot be realized in actuality, but must be satisfied indirectly, virtually, parasitically "in roundabout terms" through identification with the illicit actions of others, such as Lövborg, Diana, and Brack. Hence her wish to control the life of another, to live altogether vicariously through another. It is the best she can hope for.

Clearly, that surrogate life must be of a very special sort. Tesman does not interest her in this regard. Nor does the redeemed Lövborg. It is the dissolute

Lövborg she would control. She is not interested in Lövborg's spectacular academic achievements but only in his amours. For only those adventures supply the stimulation this *voyeur* requires. When he remarks that they have ended forever, that he has "lost [his] power of braving life out" (580), she dismisses him with the command never to return: "You must go now—and do not come here anymore" (582).

The dissolute Lövborg is, however, anathema to the proper Hedda, who is comfortable only in the company of the respectable Tesman. That supplies one motive for her gift of a gun to the distraught scholar with the advice that he use it to kill himself. She is the victim of a crippling paradox, both jailor and captive in a prison from which there is no escape. The dissolute Lövborg is necessary to satisfy the passionate Hedda and the conservative Tesman to satisfy the proper Hedda; but Lövborg is rejected by the proper Hedda and Tesman by the passionate. The bed-ridden Rina and Sheriff Elvsted's wife who also "rarely left her room" echo Hedda's isolation and paralysis, her virtual "confinement" to the rear room with its portrait of her father, her absolute dependence upon others to supply her necessary, prohibited, wants. As Ibsen reminds us through his title, although married to Jörgen Tesman she is still, inescapably, Hedda Gabler.

Hedda's conversations with Brack, who is well aware of and so repeatedly attempts to elicit her repressed sexuality, exhibit the same interior conflict. Although conscious of his intent to seduce her, which he does not conceal, she welcomes their salacious tête-à-têtes. She invites him "to be sure to call in the afternoon" (532), but threatens him with her pistol when he arrives. She verbally responds to and participates in talk of possible future intimacy; but when Brack moves towards her she backs away (536). Her past relationship with Lövborg was virtually identical. She drew from him the most intimate details of his sexual exploits. But when he proposed physical intimacy she threatened to shoot him. And indeed, it is clear that she hopes to establish with Brack a relationship similar to the one she had with Lövborg. She tells him she will not leave the "train" which imprisons her or betray her husband (539); but he is welcome to join her in her carriage—that is, to regale her with accounts of his Dionysian soirées, as Lövborg did of his escapades—and repeatedly express "in roundabout terms" his desire to bed her.

Hedda's first, private conversation with Lövborg reveals that the illicit and erotic fascinate and excite her. Their absence, and her inability to realize this aspect of self, contribute to the "boredom" of which she complains. The respectable Tesman cannot supply the necessary stimuli. With him she anticipates only interminable boredom (537.) The obvious solution would be to leave one's husband. Thea shows the way, and, incidentally, reveals that it is not society's expectations—which the conventional Thea violates without a qualm—but an inner censor that restrains Hedda.

Hedda cannot emulate Thea. Her proper self, always fearful of scandal and unwilling to admit the existence of the "other' Hedda, prohibits it. Hedda's "salvation," achieved only partly through Brack, requires for its fulfillment the return of Lövborg. She anxiously awaits his arrival, becoming animated and attentive whenever his name is mentioned. She hopes to revive in some form their past association, when he would excite and delight her with accounts of his sexual exploits, and so relieve her tedium. True to her divided nature, when in Lövborg's presence this impulse immediately encounters its contrary. Her "masculine," sensual self permits Lövborg to use the familiar "du"; her feminine, conventional self stipulates that he may, in the company of this married woman, only think it, never say it (552).

The passionate Hedda clearly craves sexual intimacy and affection—both of which she experiences vicariously. The proper Hedda rejects that same affection or love with its implication of sexual intimacy. Hence, the possibility, or more accurately in her case the "threat" of love inevitably occasions within her the impulse to destroy the one responsible, just as her admiration of Thea gave rise to the impulse to burn off her rival's beautiful hair. Love is for Hedda a "sickening word" (537; Arup: "glutinous word"). It immediately evokes denial and rejection. She tells Lövborg that it was not entirely cowardice that stayed her hand when she once threatened to shoot him. The clear implication is that love or at least affection deterred her. This was almost certainly the case, given that Hedda can only experience those emotions at such moments and in such fashion. Lövborg assumes that she has finally—if only "in roundabout terms"——revealed her love for him. But Hedda characteristically rejects that possibility. "Believe nothing of the sort!" she says (556).

In fact, the affection she refuses to concede is evident early on. It motivates her anticipation that Lövborg will win any future competition for the position Tesman seeks. If realized, this unconscious wish would commit her forever to the "genteel poverty" she loathes. "Fancy, Tesman," she says, "there will be a sort of sporting interest in that [competition]" "[H]ow can you be so indifferent," he asks. To which she replies "I am not at all indifferent. I am most eager to see who wins" (531). Given her obvious contempt for Tesman and his academic interests Hedda can mean only one thing. As the perceptive Brack observes: "Eilert Lövborg was more to you than perhaps you are willing to admit to yourself. Am I wrong?" To which Hedda, unwilling, indeed unable, to confront and acknowledge her love responds: "I don't answer such questions" (595). She need not, for Ibsen provides us with the answer. It takes the form of the burning of Lövborg's manuscript, "offspring" of his "intimacy" with Thea. The jealousy of a woman scorned motivates that act.

But the redeemed Lövborg cannot satisfy Hedda's desire for erotic adventures at second hand. He has put behind him the life that made those adventures possible. And so there must be, and in fact is, an unconscious, suppressed desire, which the proper Hedda cannot admit, to restore Lövborg to his former dissolute state, that is to ruin him, and so reestablish the only satisfying relationship of which Hedda is capable. Although the circumstances and motives differ, love and the impulse to destroy the beloved again coincide. Hedda's subsequent "gift" of the pistol with the advice Lövborg use it to kill himself is the ultimate manifestation of that "coincidence of opposites."

Hedda orders drinks served in the presence of this reformed alcoholic and suggests that he partake (549–550). Her invitation follows Thea's revelation of the "friendship" between her and Lövborg. The mere thought of her disapproval had induced Lövborg to give up his old ways, she says (525). Jealousy of Thea as of old thus enters into Hedda's scheme to resurrect the dissolute Lövborg. The impulse to control him and isolate him from Thea's redemptive influence soon surfaces as a wish to sit between them (557).

Stung by Hedda's ambivalent reception of his profession of love, which she encourages then characteristically repels, Lövborg lavishes praise upon her rival Thea, attributing to her the qualities—in particular the courage—Hedda lacks. He confirms their present and future camaraderie, and implies that Thea has taken the place of Hedda in his life: "For we two—she and I—we are two real comrades. We have absolute faith in each other; so we can sit and talk with perfect frankness" (557).

Hedda reacts as a woman scorned might—for deep within her is a love she cannot acknowledge. Once mores she proposes that Lövborg drink. When he refuses she accuses him of the cowardice he attributed to her. She challenges his resolve, urging him to attend Brack's soirée, hoping this will undo what he and Thea have accomplished and restore the familiar dissolute Lövborg, her surrogate lover, with whom she can again have an intimate relationship at second hand. When that fails to move him she reveals that Thea came to Christiania because she feared Lövborg might relapse and resume his profligate behavior. This disclosure has the intended effect. It very nearly destroys the relationship and Thea as well.

Throughout, Hedda expresses only affection for Thea, whom she would—and for the moment does—deprive of all expectations of future happiness. Yet when pressed she denies evil intent: "*Mrs. Elvsted (softly):* Oh, Hedda, Hedda—how could you do this? *Hedda: I* do it? *I*? Are you crazy?" (560). And, indeed, the proper Hedda is unaware of the envy, resentment, hatred, thwarted unexpressed love, perverse and crippling addiction to vicarious pleasure at the root of the passionate Hedda's behavior. It is revealed when Lövborg tells Thea that their "ways must part." Hedda impulsively exclaims "I knew it!" exposing the agenda that has all the while motivated her (578).

As soon as opportunity presents, Hedda again imagines Lövborg as of old "with vine leaves in his hair" ready to resume their former intimacy and fascinate her once more with tales of his sexual exploits.[10] Her unrealistic, indeed absurd expectation that because of her intervention she will again see the glorious, god-like "Dionysian" Lövborg conceals her reprehensible motive from herself and from others. That subterranean impulse is reinforce by another. Lövborg evokes forbidden desires in Hedda, and therefore, like the schoolgirl Thea, also evokes within her the impulse to destroy the person responsible for those desires. Her threat to shoot Lövborg when in the past he suggested physical intimacy, her attempt to shoot Brack who offers the same, reflect that impulse.

In Brack's case she shoots and deliberately misses, "firing in the air" (535). She threatens Lövborg but does not pull the trigger. Hence, in part, the gift of the gun with the advice that Lövborg use it to commit suicide. It is the very gun with which she shot at Brack—a bullet is missing from its chamber (596), and there is no indication that she reloads it, or has opportunity to do so. Brack identifies it: "I saw the pistol found in Lövborg's pocket, and I knew it at once as the one I had seen yesterday—and before, too" (598). And it is the same pistol with which she once threatened Lövborg:

Hedda.	No. wait! I must give you a memento to take with you. *[She goes to the writing-table and opens the drawer and the pistol-case; then returns to Lövborg with one of the pistols.]*
Lövborg (looks at her).	This? Is this the memento?
Hedda (nodding slowly).	Do you recognize it? It was aimed at you once (582).

Hedda wants Lövborg to complete the destructive act she cannot, and with the same weapon. He must accomplish this out of sight, (for, as she tells Tesman, she loathes "all sorts of ugliness and therefore "will not look upon sickness and death" [571]). She wishes to experience his death vicariously "in roundabout terms" as an act for which she was ultimately responsible, satisfying her long-held desire to control the destiny of another. Her motive is evident in her reaction to the first deceptive account of Lövborg's death. She is interested not in his possible liberation but in hers, which she thinks his sacrifice has enabled:

Hedda (in a low voice).	Oh, what a sense of freedom it gives one, this act of Eilert Lövborg's.
Brack.	Freedom, Mrs. Hedda? Well, of course, it is release for him—
Hedda.	I mean for me. It gives me a sense of freedom to know that a deed of deliberate courage is still possible in this world,—a deed of spontaneous beauty. ... Eilert Lövborg has had the courage to live his life after his own fashion. (595)

To this paralytic, who cannot "live [her] life after [her] own fashion," who therefore finds life intolerable (558) and so wishes to destroy herself but cannot, Lövborg's suicide appears "beautiful." It possesses the wholeness, coherence and finality her life lacks. He is to perform the "deed of spontaneous beauty" that eludes Hedda. His function as surrogate is to continue unto death.

Cowardice, internal conflicts and self-hatred dictate Hedda's all-encompassing incompleteness. The proper Hedda hates Brack and Lövborg because of the illicit desires they awaken (she calls Brack "hateful") and wishes to destroy them. The passionate Hedda welcomes those very desires and the men who elicit them, and so cannot destroy them. Attraction and repulsion are virtually simultaneous. The proper Hedda hates the passionate and the passionate hates the proper. Each seeks the destruction of the other.

Within a consciousness so divided and at war with itself love of another and death-dealing hatred of the beloved are inseparable and indistinguishable. That paradox is embodied by the pistol, which, as noted, represents at once Hedda's desire for and hatred of the phallus. Her gift of the deadly weapon so precious to her is an unconscious, unacknowledged love-offering by one who cannot experience affection unaccompanied by the impulse to destroy its object.

There are related, more prosaic reasons for the deadly gift. Jealousy and envy of Thea as of old, and hatred of the man who has become Thea's "comrade" as he had once been hers, also motivate it. None of those emotions—which one must attribute to the passionate Hedda—would be active lacking the love which the proper Hedda refuses to acknowledge. Hatred and love are here also inseparable. Her "gift" of the phallic pistol with the advice that Lövborg use it kill himself conceals suppressed hatred and eroticism; a desire, hidden even from herself, to annihilate the man whom she now (unconsciously) regards as an unfaithful lover.

Hedda's inner discord explains, in part, her marriage to the inconsequential Jörgen Tesman and her pregnancy. According to Julia, Hedda had many admirers, yet she chose the most conservative and conventional. The reason she gives Brack—that it was the result of her compassion for the inarticulate Tesman is clearly inadequate, as Brack in fact surmises. Hedda never expresses affection for, or even an interest in, the hapless Jörgen save when she wishes to manipulate him. She argues that Tesman was the only one who offered to "provide for" her (538) and it is clear that she means by that to keep her in luxury. But this was problematic given his straitened circumstances—his scholarship had to pay for their honeymoon—and that he had not at the time received his academic appointment. Hedda shows not the slightest interest in or apprehension about the financial difficulties that appear to be a possible consequence of Lövborg's return except as they might constrain her own extravagance. She insists upon the purchase of an expensive, unnecessary second piano which they cannot afford, and ridicules Tesman's concerns about their finances (530–31), now that a competition with Lövborg for the appointment seems likely—surely strange behavior for a woman who married to be provided for.

For an understanding of Hedda's failed relationships with her many other admirers we need look no further than her "comradeship" with the passionate Lövborg. She rejected him when their "friendship threatened to develop into something more serious" (555). Other "adorers" (538) who expressed a similar, serious intent undoubtedly suffered the same fate. As noted Hedda is incapable of normal unfettered love. She is repelled by the very word (537), fearful of possession by another and of the emotions intimacy might evoke. She required a tepid relationship with a relatively passionless, pedestrian man, into which love, on her part, need not enter, and on his part was not required of her. And that Tesman—ever grateful that the beautiful, desirable Hedda Gabler would even consider him—alone offered. Jörgen, for whom she cared not a jot, was "safe." He did not evoke in the proper Hedda the illicit, unacceptable desires experienced in the presence of Lövborg and the others.

The image of oneself as the most respectable of women—in which one preferred to believe—dictated a liaison with Jörgen Tesman, the most respectable of men. Given Hedda's dual nature, it is perfectly understandable that she despises the man she felt compelled to marry. Her sexual, masculine self necessarily despises its conservative feminine antithesis, to which the "feminine" fussy Jörgen,—raised exclusively by women as Hedda was exclusively by a man—appeals. Displaced, her self-hatred becomes hatred of Jörgen whom she unconsciously would ruin, just as she would Lövborg and Thea. That unacknowledged, unrecognized wish is manifest as indifference to her husband's financial difficulties, to the prospect that he might not receive the academic appointment which would alleviate those difficulties, and as constant, scathing criticism of poor Jörgen. As Hedda's proper self resents those who elicit forbidden desires, and so unconsciously wishes to ruin or, indeed, terminate them, so her passionate, Dionysian side would destroy those who, like Tesman, appeal to her conservative, proper side. The symmetry is perfect and pervasive.

Hedda's wish to taste at second hand delights accessible only to the male also determined her interest in Tesman. "[He] is useful precisely because he can be manipulated and dominated so unresistingly. … If anything, Tesman seems *eager* for Hedda to use him—a kind of masochist that finds the matching sadist for his need for female discipline: Hedda Dominatrix, as it were."[11] Through this weak individual, who hangs upon her every word, she might gain admittance to the male's forbidden world. A splendid house and luxurious appointments would give access to society, and so to male culture. Her desire to make of Jörgen a more acceptable surrogate prompts the hope that he go into politics. To her dismay she discovers that Tesman's interests, intellectual and familial, are purely domestic, and that they cannot afford either society or a political career.

Lövborg would have been the better choice. Of Lövborg Brack says that "his relations have a great deal of influence"—from which we can deduce they are wealthy—and that he was formerly "the hope of the family" (530). His return as the sober, successful academic apparently again in favor with his family demonstrates just what he was always capable of. That must have been evident to Hedda, just as it was to Thea. However Lövborg's advances, his obvious desire for a relationship with Hedda that involved more than mere conversation disqualified him. Hedda rejected him, indeed threatened to shoot him, when he proposed more. Unlike Thea, Hedda had no interest in redeeming Lövborg. Only the dissolute Lövborg could supply what the passionate Hedda needed. And so she encouraged, questioned, listened attentively to and, in sum, exploited the weaknesses of a man who obviously loved her and preferred even a relationship at second hand to nothing. Lövborg *had* to leave Christiania and Hedda in order to redeem himself. When he returns he again succumbs to her baleful influence.

Lövborg had whetted the appetite and aroused the desire of the passionate Hedda by his personal revelations. That forbidden desire, which the proper Hedda could not allow herself to entertain, but must attribute to the one who elicited it, led to the transformation of Lövborg into what he clearly was not. He became in her imagination a manifestation of the god Pan-Dionysus, the perfect embodiment of unbridled sensuality. She obviously would, if she could, be one of the ecstatic, frenzied Maenads who followed in the god's train. She would emulate "the huntress," Mademoiselle Diana, chaste only in name and herself just such a Maenad. However, Hedda's feminine, conservative, socially conditioned side feared what others, what "society," would say about such a relationship, feared even admitting to oneself those prohibited desires.

And so Hedda rejected Lövborg. Instead she chose the naïve Tesman, the person least associated in one's imagination with sexuality. One could have intercourse with him as required of the newly wed without admitting it to oneself or to others. Her unwillingness to accept her pregnancy is consistent with this. The proper Hedda cannot concede that she has participated in the sexual act and resents the child that reminds her of it. She associates love with that act and so rejects it too as "sickening," (537). The phallic, murderous pistol, which she turns against those who threaten her with sex, suggests the feelings evoked in her by the male organ.

Hedda sleeps in a separate bedroom upon returning from her honeymoon (v. 508, "Hedda's bedroom"). Since she clearly controls the living arrangements that is probably at her insistence. She wears a loose gown to conceal her true condition from others—and from herself. She resents Julia's repeated allusions to her pregnancy and terminates all conversation when it veers in that direction. Given her scorn of Jörgen, and her aversion to love—with its implications of physical intimacy—and to her pregnancy, one must assume that Hedda rarely participated in the sexual act. For that reason, too, she denies her pregnancy. She prefers to think it unlikely. Tesman may be a narrow pedant, but he is not an utter idiot. His otherwise incomprehensible "ignorance" of Hedda's condition—clearly evident to Julia and Brack—probably reflects the infrequency of their intercourse. He also thinks pregnancy unlikely. His observation that the two empty rooms in the villa will serve for his library (508) suggests that he does not anticipate children—or sex—in the future. He expects that Hedda—who married the worshipful, dependent Jörgen, in part because it enabled her to control and limit their sexual relationship—will remain remote and inaccessible, a conclusion that her obvious scorn of him confirms. Brack suspects indifferent love-making: "You have never gone through any really stimulating experience," he says (544). Tesman's disappointment is evident in his frequent "accidental" use of the maiden name of his "old flame," Thea. He unconsciously desires to reestablish the intimacy lacking in his wedded life and in the end openly does so, abandoning his new wife to the libertine Brack whose predatory intent he must suspect.

If the proper Hedda is averse to sex or indeed to physical contact; the passionate is not. She is subject to all of the normal sexual impulses. They cannot be satisfied of course; her "other" self prohibits it. But they exist nonetheless, manifesting themselves early on as the desire to experience the illicit and forbidden at one remove, "in roundabout terms," and subsequently as jealousy, envy and hatred of the women who possess the only male that fascinates her. She is overcome, victimized by those emotions.

Hedda's jealousy, as well as her hatred of self, of Thea and of the "unfaithful" Lövborg motivate her burning of the manuscript. Lövborg's devotion to her rival, whom he regards as the "mother" of their literary "child," which, in his words, contains "Thea's pure soul" (582) deeply offends her. The barren Thea was able to achieve the intimacy and conceive the "child" that the fertile Hedda could not. Thea and Lövborg had in her presence referred to his purported destruction of the manuscript as "child-murder." (580). And Hedda clearly regards its actual destruction as precisely that:

Hedda *(throws one of the quires in the fire, and whispers to herself)*.	Now I am burning your child, Thea!——Burning it, curly-locks! Your child and Eilert Lövborg's. (*Throws the rest in.*) I am burning—I am burning your child (583)

That passionate exclamation refutes the assumption that Hedda's intent is simply to advance her husband's career. Thea has destroyed the "old" Lövborg so essential for Hedda's vicarious sexual pleasures. "She has broken my courage and my power of braving life out," he says (580). To their beloved "child" born of the merging of souls, Hedda must surely contrast her own hated offspring, the result of a physical coupling which she regards as "sickening" with a man whom she scorns. She cannot admit to herself that she desires her unborn child's disappearance or death. The proper Hedda forbids it. But that is clearly the case given that she is unwilling to even acknowledge its existence. Her unconscious "agenda" requires Thea's ruin, Lövborg's death, and the death of their "child" and hers. The burning of the manuscript makes the first two more probable, insures the third, and serves as surrogate for the last. She burns not only Thea and Lövborg's "child" but "in roundabout terms" her own.

The depth and intensity of Hedda's jealousy, envy and hatred (emotions which this woman whose "*steel-grey eyes express a cold unruffled repose*" cannot consciously concede) becomes apparent when we consider that simply by returning the manuscript to Lövborg she could have revived his faith in himself and put an end to his thoughts of self-destruction. The reappearance of the "child" that formerly united Lovborg and Thea would, however, almost certainly have restored their shattered relationship. And that the passionate Hedda cannot permit. She therefore destroys the essential document, irrevocably prohibiting a positive outcome for the two.

Lövborg "was found shot—in Mademoiselle Diana's boudoir" (596). Brack's account of his death allows either "an accidental shot or murder" (599). Hedda's pistol was still in Lövborg's breast-pocket, where he had placed it after she gave it to him, missing only the bullet she had earlier fired at Brack. As we have noted, there is no indication that Hedda reloads it or has opportunity to do so. Brack asserts that "The ball had lodged … in the bowels" (596). If there had been an accidental discharge while the pistol was still in Lövborg's pocket his garments surely would have revealed it; for the bullet would have had to traverse his pocket and his clothed torso. Brack's speculates that Diana tore the gun from Lövborg's hand, shot him and then replaced it in his pocket. He does not mention a third option: that Lövborg's death might have been the work of the pistol-carrying Mademoiselle Diana herself (526) who used her own weapon. Unafraid to take the action the "cowardly" Hedda could not, she is, as it were, the very apotheosis of the passionate Hedda, the woman Hedda would or might have been, were she not prohibited by her other, proper adversarial self.

Ibsen provides us with adequate motives for Diana's murderous action. They are similar to the jealousy and envy which contribute to Hedda's gift of the pistol. Diana's presence in Christiania is not accidental. She has returned to be with her old lover, who has also recently returned and whom she invites to her soirée (573) hoping to reestablish their relationship. His subsequent persistent attempts to find in her boudoir his missing "child," which she naturally assumes to be the result of an affair with another, enrages this passionate woman, who had threatened to shoot Lövborg once before for abandoning her (526). Ibsen's ambiguous language leaves open the possibility that Diana shoots Lövborg in or near the groin (*underlivet*), which would, of course be appropriate both for Diana, committed to the sensual, and for the "proper" Hedda, who rejects it. It would also confirm the association of pistol and phallus.

Now Hedda knows the history of the pistol. She saw Lövborg place it in his breast-pocket where it was found after his death, suggesting that he had never used it. She therefore has good cause to assume that Diana shot Lövborg, and also to conclude that he accepted her "love-gift" not because he actually intended suicide, but rather to confront the well-armed Diana on equal terms and demand from her the return of his "child" and Thea's. She very nearly admits this when Brack tells her that soon after Lövborg left her he returned to Diana's talking "wildly about a lost child." "Ah—so that was why—[he wanted the pistol]" she says (596).

Were Hedda to assert that her pistol was stolen—as Brack suggests—or should it be established that Diana had used her own pistol, and should the ownership of the pistol found in Lövborg's pocket remain a mystery, it would eliminate any possibility of Hedda's direct involvement in Lövborg's death and of blackmail by Brack. However, when the details of the affair became public it would appear that Lövborg had previously been devoted to his Dionysian mistress, the seductive Diana, and at the time of his death was in love with Thea, in fact risking his life to recover their lost "child." It would establish the supremacy, and confirm the "narrative," of Hedda's rivals. They determined the course of a life she strove to control. Most importantly, it would eliminate her love-gift and long "intimacy" with Lövborg from the equation. And that concession is anathema to the passionate Hedda who in her conflicted way loved the dissolute scholar, and was committed to their unique relationship. In an outburst impossible for the proper Hedda, her "other" self impetuously and violently denies that Lövborg might have stolen the pistol: "Stolen it! That is not true! He did not steal it!" (596). "Death rather than [admit] that," she says (599).

As Brack justly observes, fear of scandal prohibits the proper Hedda from publicly acknowledging that she deliberately gave Lövborg the pistol. Any such admission might eventually result in the revelation, or at least the intimation, of motives which the proper Hedda regards as reprehensible. Should she appear in court, she would be put in the humiliating position of explaining her "inexplicable" behavior before her victorious rivals, who would surely be there. Brack correctly notes that "you will have to answer the question: "Why did you give Eilert Lövborg the pistol? And what conclusions will people draw from the fact that you did give it to him?" (598). Did she give the pistol to Lovborg so that he could threaten Diana? So that he could kill himself? Was she perhaps in love with the dead man? Whatever her answer Hedda would be forever compromised. Her unique relationship to Lövborg and her ignominious defeat in the contest for his affection might very well be revealed.

Brack's silence would enable the passionate Hedda to avoid the unacceptable alternative of falsifying the truth, and the proper Hedda to avoid the equally unacceptable alternative of admitting the truth, but at the expense of "sickening" sexual servitude to the judge. Hedda is trapped. This supplies one motive for her suicide. But there are others.

Hedda will soon bear a child she detests and become responsible for its upbringing. The hated Thea, Tesman's "old flame," now possesses her husband, whom she will, like Lövborg, "inspire" (600) and with whom—as Hedda has good cause to suspect—Tesman will eventually have the sexual relationship Hedda has denied him. Thea is barren and so there will be no inconvenient consequences. As Arthur Ganz remarks: "It is hard to avoid the suggestion in the tableau of Thea and Tesman happily at work in reconstructing Lövborg's manuscript that Ibsen points toward a future relationship …"[12] The two will resurrect the "child" Hedda thought she had destroyed, which will then become *their* beloved "offspring." The scorned Tesman has rejected her. To cite Mervyn Nicholson, "he literally consigns Hedda to Brack—'you go and sit down again, now, with Mr. Brack'—as if throwing her away. His casual dismissal is, in the context of play, an appalling snub …."[13] Hedda asks, "Is there nothing I can do to help you two?" Her husband replies, with chilling effect, "No, nothing in the world" (600). Tesman will spend his evenings with Thea at Julia's, abandoning this proud woman to the mercies of Brack, who will repeatedly attempt to force upon her the sexual relationship the proper Hedda finds repulsive. The scandal which the proper Hedda dreads will inevitably be the consequence of her husband's betrayal and her would-be lover's blackmail.

Suicide is the perfect, inevitable ending to this tragic tale of inner warfare between competing selves, each of which seeks to annihilate the other. The hatred that Hedda has directed at others, her desire for revenge, recoils, becoming what it truth it always was—the attack of self upon self. Ibsen represents the disjuncture of mind and body always implicit in this relation, and the proper Hedda's rejection of the physical, by having her appear at the end with her body concealed by a curtain. Only her apparently severed head is seen by the audience. The bodily, passionate Hedda, entirely concealed by the curtains as she was nearly always concealed in fact, is manifest only as the "wild dance" Hedda plays behind the closed curtains on the hidden ancestral piano immediately before she shoots herself. Division and inner conflict persist until the very end. They are indeed responsible for that end.

There were two weapons in Hedda's pistol-case, one belonging to her and another belonging to her deceased father; but they were not identical. Brack has no trouble identifying the specific pistol with which Hedda threatened him, and Hedda expects Lövborg to do the same. We must assume the pistol was distinctive. Moreover, it is virtually certain it was Hedda's own pistol, with which she learned to shoot. That pistol, her personal prized possession, was her "love-offering" to Lövborg. The police now have it. Therefore, of necessity, she uses the remaining pistol, her father's, to kill herself. And this is just, as is the fact that her suicide occurs beneath the ever watchful eyes of her deceased parent. For it is the latter's pernicious, continuing influence, the suppressed, destructive sexuality for which he was responsible, and which the pistol aptly symbolizes, that leads to Hedda's tragic end.

None of the men who admire or desire Hedda can understand this proud, complex, tormented creature, who fully expresses her agony and destructive impulses only when alone. They remain ignorant of her nature and so of the true causes of her death. Tesman responds with the dismissive and ineffectual "Fancy that!" (Arup: "Think of that!"). The judicious Brack, who prides himself on his insights into Hedda's character and assumes he offers her the unencumbered sexual relationship she has always desired, is flabbergasted: "Good God! People don't do such things," he says (601). Her death behind the closed curtain, out of sight of the others, emphasizes their ignorance of her and her utter isolation from all. Hedda herself, inwardly discordant and divided as she is, cannot comprehend the impulses that led to this cul-de-sac. Was her suicide motivated by heroism or cowardice? Did the passionate Hedda triumph, or did the proper Hedda, fearful of disclosure and enforced intimacy? Neither she nor we can say. The drama appropriately ends on an autumnal evening heralding the approach of the prolonged winter darkness symbolic of the ignorance of all.

Notes

1. Hermann J. Weigand, *Modern Ibsen* 248.
2. John Northam, *Critical Study*, 185.
3. James McFarlane, *Four Major Plays*, xi.
4. Caroline W. Mayerson in Fjelde, *Critical Essays*, 138.
5. Stein Haugom Olsen, "Why Does Hedda Gabler Marry Jørgen Tesman?," 605.
6. Arthur Ganz, "Miracle and Vine Leaves," 11.
7. Elizabeth Jacobs, "Henrik Ibsen and the Doctrine of Self-Realization," 427.
8. Stein Haugom Olson, "Why Does Hedda Gabler Marry Jörgen Tesman?," 598–599.
9. Evert Sprinchorn, "The unspoken text in *Hedda Gabler*," 356.

10. Sprinchorn traces this image to Nietzsche who "described his Goethean superman as a 'highly cultured human being who keeping himself in check and having reverence for himself dares to allow himself the whole compass and wealth of natural being—a man to whom nothing is forbidden except *weakness*.'" "The Unspoken Text in *Hedda Gabler*," 362.
11. Mervyn Nicholson, "L'Homme Fatal in *Hedda Gabler*," 366.
12. Arthur Ganz, "Miracle and Vine Leaves,"12.
13. Mervyn Nicholson, "L'Homme Fatal in *Hedda Gabler*," 374.

References

All parenthetical page citations in this text are from *Eleven Plays of Henrik Ibsen*, ed. B. A. Cerf, D. S. Klopfer. New York: *The Modern Library*, 1935. Translators not given but those of plays discussed in this volume appear to be R. Farquharson Sharp (*Ghosts*, *An Enemy of the People*), Edmund Gosse and William Archer (*The Master Builder*, *Hedda Gabler*), and William Archer (*The Wild Duck*). I found those older translations satisfactory for my purposes. In the few cases where translation appeared to be an issue I have appended parallel citations from *The Oxford Ibsen* (*Ibsen* (McFarlane, James Walter, ed. and trans. *The Oxford Ibsen*, 8 vols. London: Oxford University Press, 1962).

Fjelde, Rolf, ed. *Ibsen: A Collection of Critical Essays*. Englewood Cliffs, NJ: Prentice-Hall, 1965.

Ganz, Arthur. "Miracle and Vine Leaves: An Ibsen Play Rewrought." *PMLA* 94, no. 1 (January 1979): 9–21.

Jacobs, Elizabeth. "Henrik Ibsen and the Doctrine of Self-Realization." *The Journal of English and Germanic Philology* 38, no. 3 (July 1939): 416–430.

McFarlane, James and Jens Arup trans. *Henrik Ibsen, Four Major Plays*. *Oxford World's Classics*. Oxford, England: Oxford University Press, 2008.

Nicholson, Mervyn. "L'Homme Fatal in *Hedda Gabler*." *Modern Drama* 35, no. 3 (Fall 1992): 365–377.

Northam, John. *Ibsen, A Critical Study*. Cambridge: Cambridge University Press, 1973.

Olsen, Stein Haugom. "Why Does Hedda Gabler Marry Jørgen Tesman?" *Modern Drama* 28, no. 4 (Winter 1985): 591–610.

Sprinchorn, Evert. "The Unspoken Text in *Hedda Gabler*." *Modern Drama* 36, no. 3 (Fall 1993): 353–367.

Weigand, Hermann J. *The Modern Ibsen*. New York: Henry Holt & Co., 1925.

· 5 ·

THE MASTER BUILDER

Prefatory

Brain Downs observes that "A great deal of personal experience went to the composition of *The Master Builder*." In support of this thesis, he reviews Ibsen's relations with Emily Bardach, Helene Raff, Hildur Andersen and Laura Kieler.[1] "The final question of this order," he says is, "How far, if at all, should Ibsen be identified with Halvard Solness?"[2] He concludes that the answer to that question, however interesting in itself, is ultimately irrelevant to our interpretation of the play, which is, after all, about Solness, not Ibsen:

> Ibsen's plays are subjective expressions of his personal emotions and sentiments. … On the other hand the objectivity of *The Master Builder* must not be denied. Ibsen would never permit the 'reality' of his figures and stories to be called in question; … For *The Master Builder* was and remains the story, as Mr. Desmond McCarthy has put it, of an 'elderly architect who falls off his scaffold while trying to show off before a young lady'. The tragedy attached to the fable is that of the sick conscience caught in an *impasse*; and it is not in itself affected by the question whether the sick conscience presented is that of the author in disguise or whether he conceived it purely through the strength of his imagination.[3]

Ibsen depicts an aging artist at the end of his tether. His powers are failing. He is dependent upon others for whatever success he enjoys. Clients have begun to abandon him. It is folly to assume that Solness is a "stand in" for Ibsen whose creativity was at its zenith when he composed *The Master Builder*. Ibsen's few comments support this conclusion. He clearly regarded Solness as an independent being who resembled him in certain respects but not at all in others. Their "admixture" in Solness produced a unique creature very different from its creator. The defining characteristic of Solness—his fear of the younger generation—was completely absent in Ibsen:

> [Solness] was a man who was somewhat akin to me. I am, however, not afraid of youth. I have never been afraid of youth. I knew it would come and beat upon the door. It came, and I greet it now with pleasure.[4]

I heartily agree with Downs' conclusion that "the play's the thing," not the biography of the author. I would add to it certain observations of T. S. Eliot's. He speaks specifically of the poet's methodology, but his remarks apply to all literary artists of the first rank:

> When a poet's mind is perfectly equipped for its work, it is constantly amalgamating disparate experience; the ordinary man's experience is chaotic, irregular, fragmentary. The latter falls in love, or reads Spinoza, and these experiences have nothing to do with each other, or with the noise of the typewriter or the smell of cooking; in the mind of the poet these experiences are always forming new wholes.[5]

In "Tradition and the Individual Talent" Eliot compares the poet's sensibility to a chemical catalyst that causes two disparate elements to combine to produce a third compound very different from its contributory elements. The catalyst itself remains unchanged. That, too, seems to me applicable to the case at hand. One's experiences are not irrelevant. They afford the necessary ingredients, the "elements" upon which the "catalyst" of the dramatist's sensibility acts. However they are not, and must not, be confused with the results of that operation. The critic's proper concern—whether his subject-matter is poetry or drama—is the unique modification and fusion of such experiences or "elements" that occurs in the art work, transforming them into a new and very different whole with very different properties that belong *only* to the art work, *not* to the larger world, which of course includes the biography or "experience" of the author.

Weigand's analysis of *The Master Builder* affords an interesting test of this thesis. He goes to great lengths to find parallels between Ibsen and Solness. But when all is said he interprets the play as the encounter of an aging paranoid with a manipulative young woman suffering from arrested sexual development who is in quest of an orgasm as "thrilling" as the one experienced in his company ten years earlier.[6]

As for the master builder's alleged "paranoia" it is, like the peculiarities of other protagonists in the plays we have considered, simply the result of the author's intensification of perfectly ordinary characteristics shared by all of mankind. The artistic "operation" here is akin to Shakespeare's intensification of Othello's jealously and Iago's envy. Shakespeare doubtless experienced jealousy and envy. But the functions of those emotions in *Othello* are necessarily unique and very different from their functions in the life of its creator. As we have observed, the simultaneous existence of the polarities respectability—prurience within one personality is not confined to Hedda. However, in Hedda those antitheses are extreme. Nor would Ibsen have had to look far to find perfectly normal individuals "thrilled" like Hilde at the prospect of another's possibly disastrous fall from a height. He would only have to visit the circus with its trapeze artists and high-wire acts and observe the audience or consult his own feelings. The impulse to destroy, to ruin, the beloved is common enough. It can be provoked by the conviction that one has been betrayed, by jealousy, by envy, by rejection. The newspapers afford ample examples of that impulse in action. *Othello*, *Hedda*, and, as we hope to demonstrate, *The Master Builder* afford instances of it intensified and transmuted into one element of an artistic whole.

Like Dr. Thomas Stockmann, Solness is "infected" with consuming egotism. He has ruthlessly exploited family, business associates and the younger generation of architects in his quest for supremacy. His "paranoid" fear of retribution is a manifestation of well-deserved guilt that cannot be completely suppressed. "The fear which [Solness] suffers in high places is defined, through metaphor, as conscience; he fears recrimination. The height of the tower is freedom from obligation to others, a boundless self-satisfaction, a sense of the will as ultimate agency."[7] Ibsen's metaphor implies that the ascent and the fear are inseparable. It is precisely the "sense of the will as ultimate agency" that recoils as "fear of recrimination." There is nothing abnormal in this, unless one believes that conscience and egotism and their conflicting demands are abnormal. Their extreme manifestations in *The Master Builder*, like the jealousy of Othello, are indispensable if they are to function as elements in the esthetic whole. The myths promulgated by Solness—of trolls, devils, and of a God who takes a unique interest in him—reflect his attempts to reconcile two irreconcilable premises: that only he should build and that he is not guilty of the evils this conviction occasions.

The master builder's reluctance to accept responsibility for wrongdoing is hardly unique. In Solness, however, the conflict of conscience with the need to impose one's will is extreme. If we inappropriately assume actual madness, we obscure the critical moral issue; the agent is no longer responsible for his wrongs. And, in fact, Solness offers this attractive alternative to Herdal early in the play. It is but one of the many devices he employs to avoid responsibility for his actions.

....

The Master Builder explores a number of the issues raised by its predecessors: the pernicious effects of egotism; self-destructive inner conflict; self-deception and its consequence—the inability to distinguish truth from dream or illusion. It differs in that this failing is depicted as inseparable from one's highest aspirations and greatest achievements. And so at the play's conclusion we paradoxically experience simultaneous victory and defeat.

The work affords many instances of the "inconsistencies" and inner divisions noted in earlier plays. All can be traced to the protagonists' refusal to acknowledge difficult truths. They substitute instead rationalizations or fantasies. Like Hilde they build "Castles in the air" (369).

To "build" is, in this instance, to "will" into existence what one *would* have exist. Witnesses to the same event, Ragnar perceives failure ("So, after all, he could not do it"), Hilde victory ("But he mounted right to the top. And I heard harps in the air") (383). Each sees what he or she *would* see. As in *Ghosts*, truth is elusive, ambiguous—for the audience or reader as well as for the protagonists. In view of Ibsen's association of light with truth and darkness with falsehood this may in part account for the dating of critical events in *The Master Builder* to the "ambiguous" time of the equinox when neither day nor night prevails.

Secular, elevated man-made structures and mountain peaks here symbolize not only "freedom from obligation to others," as Lyons notes, but the wish to be "above" or superior to them. They are associated in this play with egotists who think themselves exempt from human limitations. Solness' construction of a tower attached to his home rather than to the church affirms his dream of secular, egocentric supremacy. Hilde's sojourn in the mountains, her dream of inhabiting a tower higher than any other, have much the same significance. To that affirmation Ibsen opposes the inferior, unyielding quarry rocks that shatter Solness's head, site of dreaming. He clearly represents the type in which egocentric dream and adamantine reality tragically collide.

Hilde Wangel is almost completely immersed in her waking dream, and therefore nearly immune to the "collision" that always threatens and eventually destroys Solness. We cannot know whether what she asserts about events at Lysanger accurately describes them, is a dream that has become for her the sole reality, or is a fiction deliberately invented by this destitute woman to insure a place in the Solness household: "the quality of [her] experience is never specifically defined as the memory of an actual event, a fantasy, a lie, or a delusion."[8] For ten years she has nurtured a desire for a "kingdom" based upon her "recollection" of an intimate encounter with Solness about which they disagree and which may never have occurred. Hilde was then a young girl when the imagination is most active. Ten years later she is still in many ways a child with a child's ability to transfigure reality in the imagination and a child's selfish impulses. Ibsen signifies this by having her sleep in the nursery. The next morning she observes that she slept "Like a child in a cradle" (333). Dreaming appeals to her as an escape from reality. She thinks it "delicious to lie and dream" and dreams "Almost always" (314). As she says in the last act: "If one could only sleep the whole thing away" (366). "You must have dreamt all this," protests Solness, when Hilde tells him that at Lysanger he kissed her "many times" (319).

Her greatest fear is that reality will not coincide with her dreams. Her evaluation of Solness, either as he was in the past or as he now appears to be, cannot be taken at face value. She is less interested in what Solness *is* than in what he *must be* to satisfy her childhood dream and exalted view of her own destiny. When confronted with facts that threaten her dream she rejects them. When Solness tells her that heights make him dizzy she replies, "Don't tell me you can ever be dizzy!" (358). When he asserts that he must in the end fall before the onslaught of the "younger generation" "*putting her hands over her ears*" she refuses to listen (353). When Ragnar tells her that Solness is too cowardly to ascend the tower her response is "*violent and uncontrolled.*" "I *will* see it!" she says, "I *will* and *must* see it!" (372). She rejects Ragnar's explanation that Solness kept him solely to keep Kaja. For ten years she has nurtured the illusion—which we know to be false—that Solness cared only for her. ("All these ten years I have believed in you so utterly—so utterly," she says [378].) "No," she tells Ragnar, "I will tell you why he kept hold of her":

Hilde.	In order to keep hold of you.
Ragnar.	Has he told you so?
Hilde.	No, but it is so. It *must* be so! (*Wildly.*) I will—I *will* have it so! (371–372)

When reality threatens, Hilde instinctively retreats to her dream world. Although she wishes to remain with Solness she regretfully concludes she must leave for the sake of Aline: "I cannot do harm to anyone I know," she says. Soon after she remarks, "Oh if one could only sleep the whole thing away!" (365–367). She then "*lays her arms flat on the table, rests the left side of her head on her hands and shuts her eyes,*" as if dreaming. She confesses that return to her father would be return to a "cage" this "wild bird" cannot endure. Solness wants her to stay notwithstanding the pain he knows it will cause his wife. He reminds her of her enthusiasm for the Viking spirit and for the "robust conscience" of those who take what they want without regard for others. Hilde then "*sits erect on the bench, with animation. Her eyes have once more the sparkling expression of gladness*" (367). Reverting to her dream, she demands her imaginary "castle," her "castle in the air." Dreaming of that castle "*Her expression becomes more and more veiled. She seems gazing inwards at herself*" (368).

Although Solness's tragic accident is clearly visible Hilde does not immediately perceive it because she does not want to. The crowd cries, "his whole head is crushed—he fell straight into the quarry." Hilde turns to Ragnar and says ("*quietly*," the stage directions tell us) "I can't see him up there now" (383). Even after this catastrophe she will not acknowledge the collapse of her dream but still acclaims "her" master builder. Like Gregers who does not "see" the repaired gift of deed on the table before him, she perceives only what she wishes to perceive.

We could attribute her unusual behavior to "arrested [sexual] development"—adolescent infatuation persisting into adulthood—or to some other psychological defect. As noted, that is Weigand's argument.[9] And Downs observes that Hilde's stay in a sanatorium—where she met Aline—argues for pathological instability.[10] But the pattern of the drama as a whole contradicts such explanations. For, as we shall observe, Hilde's commitment to illusion is characteristic of all in this play.

Her repressed, unconscious fear that actuality may in the end defeat her accounts for her strange, recurrent dream in which she imagines herself falling with legs tucked up, a dream which she shares with Solness, who has the same fear (333). Should her waking dreams prove baseless, without "a firm foundation" in Solness's words (379), she will "fall." One tucks up one's legs to forestall as long as possible contact with the unyielding reality that threatens to destroy one's dreams. The image anticipates subsequent references to the biblical Fall and to the master-builder's tragic death. Lesser "fall" can represent greater. For like the latter it is the consequence of the man and woman's egotistical dreams of supremacy.

Hilde's nearly complete immersion in her waking, or conscious, dream of supremacy, interposes a barrier between this young woman and her nocturnal dreams of self-destruction. Unlike the aging Solness, she cannot readily imagine her own end—the final, destructive collision of one's dreams with adamantine reality. She finds the same dream of falling that terrifies him "tremendously thrilling" (333).

She shares with Solness not only the dream of falling, but also egotism, an exaggerated sense of self importance, signified by the elevation that precedes the fall. Her desire for dominion over others is manifest as fondness for heights, for mountaineering. In fantasy she associates her role as princess with life in the very highest of towers where she can "look down on the other people—on those who are building churches, and homes for mother and father and the troop of children …" (368). Her egotism dictates the priority of her dream. It requires that she impose it upon the master builder. In her cosmos there is "room" for only *one* dream—*her* dream of a "Kingdom" which this "princess" rules from a dizzying height—just as in his there is only "room" for *his* dream; the dream that inspired the tower of his new home; the dream of one plagued by self-doubt and failing powers, who *would* nonetheless domineer. Belief in the power of will is characteristic of both protagonists. One *wills* the dream into existence. One's will allows one to control others to facilitate this.

Hilde's name and sailor's accoutrements identify her as the Hilde Wangel of Ibsen's *Lady from the Sea*. That Hilde is fascinated by the ambitious dreams of the sculptor Lyngstrand, who is destined to die before they are realized (a fact unknown to him but known to her). She draws Lyngstrand out, encourages his futile dreaming. She finds it "exciting" that "He believes it all so firmly and is so intensely happy over it. And yet it will never come to pass, never in the world!"

We detect here an unconscious wish to be superior to or "above" another; a need to impose one's will upon this person. In this case it takes the relatively mild form of deliberately eliciting and encouraging Lyngstrand's dreams, all the while possessing god-like knowledge of the fatal illness that will prevent their realization. In effect Hilde controls the dreamer, just as she later does the master builder. As this example indicates, the young Hilde is also fascinated by and attracted to the death that annihilates dream and dreamer. That, too, is unconscious. What surfaces in consciousness is not the fatal, impermissible death wish, but a certain thrill or *frisson* when contemplating, or in the presence of, danger to the dreamer.

The mature Hilde of *The Master Builder* exhibits the same inclinations, and the same inner division between conscious and unconscious. As McFarlane notes, "Like the Hilde Wangel of *The Lady from the Sea* she is thrilled and excited by any hint of the encroachment of death upon life."[11] In her, affection and admiration, the need to dominate and the impulse to destroy, or bear witness to destruction, are inseparable.

"Was anyone burnt?" Hilde asks "*excitedly*" when Solness speaks of the fire in the old house (339). His plan to neglect the crack in the flue and so bring about the catastrophe that will establish him is for her "thrilling" (346). Consciously in awe of the master builder whom she worships, she nonetheless finds it "wonderfully thrilling" to contemplate the possibility of his death. "Fancy, if he should fall over! He—the master builder himself!" (316). Her wild behavior years before when Solness appeared about to realize *his* dream, and place the wreath at Lysanger nearly resulted in just such a catastrophe. It was not simply childish thoughtlessness, but emanated from deep within her being. We know this because Hilde later repeats the very same gesture, this time with fatal consequences, although now fully aware of the danger, having been warned of it by Solness (316), Aline (357, 373), and Herdal (380). As before she was dressed in white, so now she waves Aline's white shawl, "snatched" from Herdal without his consent as if to be certain that the deadly circumstances are repeated precisely. The evidence available to her clearly indicates that this action could result in the death of Solness. One must assume that unconsciously she desires that result, notwithstanding her devotion to the master builder. *Complete* domination of another implies control unto death. Hilde's final exultant "My master builder" expresses its fulfillment. Her comparison of herself to a bird of prey that kills to possess is quite accurate save in one respect: this bird of prey requires a willing victim; she is otherwise impotent.

For, excepting her questionable and perhaps imaginary recollection of a childhood encounter with Solness, Hilde's dictatorial, domineering manner has no basis in fact. It reflects her reluctance to acknowledge difficult truths, very similar to the reluctance noted in other protagonists we have studied. Hilde is destitute and homeless. "I shall never go home again," (349), she says. She possesses only what she brings with her and that is virtually nothing. Her straitened circumstances suggest a difficult, perhaps unpleasant departure from home, possibly the result of parental rejection. Her physical dependency upon others' generosity (she lacks clothing and money; cf. 313, "I have no trunk," and 315, "I have run through all my money") reflects her spiritual dependency. Her desire to reign as a "princess" looking down upon her inferior subjects expresses all that is lacking in her life. She is the antithesis of that person. In fact she has *only* her dream, and the hope that Solness will realize it.

Because of her complete dependency, and her reluctance to acknowledge that dependency, Hilde is abnormally sensitive to rejection, imagined or real. And that is what she perceives. Her subterranean, destructive impulses are reinforced by what she regards as the master builder's neglect of her at the expiration of their ten-year separation. All those years she trusted Solness "utterly" (378), and was "furious" when he did not fulfill his promise (354). "[Y]ou didn't come—as you promised me" she says (321). Her resentment is justified even if the occasion for it is imaginary. Solness clearly forgot her. She has, moreover, to contend with his apparent commitment to Aline. In Hilde's presence he indicates that he has built the new house, or "castle" with its tower, for Aline, telling his wife "Now all you have to do is to think about moving into our new home—as quickly as you can," (356). But Hilde believes that it was promised *her* ten years earlier:

Solness (approaches her).	You might have the topmost room in the tower, Hilde—there you might live like a princess.
Hilde (indefinably, between earnest and jest).	Yes, that is what you promised me.
Solness.	Did I really?
Hilde.	Fie, Mr. Solness! You said I should be a princess, and that you would give me a kingdom. (357–358)

Hilde is clearly capable of jealousy. Her wish to have Solness sign Ragnar's plans reflects not only the reasons which she gives but one which she does not—namely the need to rid herself of Kaja, a possible rival for the master builder's affection. She knows that Ragnar and Kaja are engaged (314, 344). She assumes that once Ragnar can build for himself he and Kaja will marry and depart.

Shortly before Solness begins his fatal ascent, Hilde learns from a conversation with Ragnar that Solness and Kaja may very well have been intimate, possibly still are, and that Kaja plans to remain with Solness, notwithstanding her dismissal by him (371). When Solness proposes to join her in their "castle" Hilde asks "*with an expression of repressed resentment*," "Only with me? Will there be no others to the party? … that Kaja at the desk … don't you want to take her with you too?" Solness does not firmly exclude the possibility. "I will not answer such a question," he says. "You must believe in me wholly and entirely" (378). He appears to be devoted to, if tormented by, the wife towards whom he feels a "boundless debt." Will she, too, be a member of the party? Solness repeatedly questions Hilde's veracity, the validity of her dream. For one so self-absorbed that too, is cause for "*repressed resentment.*" Hilde clearly has reason to resent, even to hate the master builder whom she worships.

And so to Hilde's innate sadistic impulses and fascination with death, we must add a series of very real affronts that exacerbate those tendencies. Her hostility, springing from the aforementioned sources, from behavior similar to, but more intense than our circus goers', from the compulsion of this "bird of prey" to take from others what she wants for herself, and from an innate desire to "rule" or control another completely, accounts in part for the fact that she compels Solness to approve Ragnar's plans, although he insists it will be the ruin of him (352–353); that she does not tell Solness Aline mourns not her children, but her dolls, a revelation that surely would lighten the burden of guilt of which he complains; that she finds the prospect of Solness's hazardous ascent, which she urges upon him, "fearfully thrilling"(370); that at the moment of his apparent triumph she appears to anticipate his death ("it is finished" [382] were Christ's penultimate words [John 19.30]); and that immediately after this remark she distracts Solness and so precipitates his fatal fall.

Her egocentric dream dictates that Solness be committed to her alone. Only his death while subservient to her will can accomplish this. And that is what she achieves. Consciously she wishes Solness to succeed; her dream requires that. Unconsciously she wishes him to fail. For success could well be followed by unacceptable relationships with Kaja and Aline. In time there might be other women. "Her" master builder would no longer be hers. Solness's simultaneous success and failure (for he does climb and does place the wreath, yet falls) satisfies both conscious and unconscious desires.

Hilde's complex, ambiguous behavior is not unique. Aline both created and destroyed her children, and Solness "crushed" those for whom it was his dream to build "Cosy, comfortable, bright homes; where father and mother and the whole troop of children live in safety and gladness …" (341). Ragnar's dream of greatness, shared by his desolate father, is inseparable from their desire to ruin Solness, to crush him as he crushed them; and Kaja's dream of union with Solness requires her betrayal of Ragnar, whom she intends to marry. Even Herdal is not exempt. We shall observe that this cheerful, smiling physician whose business it is to preserve life, envies and resents Solness, and therefore abandons him precisely when most needed, contributing to his death.

Hilde thinks herself the exponent and defender of the dream in which she rules like a "princess" in a high tower, and the liberator of Solness, presently chained to a "dead woman," who will "rule" at her side; and so, superficially, she appears; for that is the dream in which she consciously believes. Beneath it, in the unconscious, resides a different, difficult, disconcerting reality ultimately fatal to the master builder. It is symbolized by the "very dirty" underclothes, worn next to the skin and concealed from outward view, which this superficially vigorous, healthy, attractive woman carries in her knapsack (312). They represent the baggage or burden of devious, suppressed, death-dealing impulses she brings with her. Hilde's stay at the same sanatorium that accommodated Aline suggests a similar distinction between superficial "health" and concealed "disease" (312).

Obedient to unacknowledged resentment and destructive impulses, her memory, is unusually selective—a characteristic she also shares with the other protagonists—and facilitates the necessary metamorphosis of reality. She refuses to entertain the thought that Solness, moved by her will, can fail, and so "forgets" his warning that once before she almost caused his death by distracting him when he was placing a wreath. Nor will she concede that Ragnar has sufficient ability to challenge him. That would diminish the stature of "her" master builder, and, by implication, the importance of the dream in which he figures. As if to establish Ragnar's insignificance she cannot recall his name (352).

But the impulse to reshape reality goes beyond mere lapses of memory. Hilde reinvents the past when it is in her interest to do so. The drama affords several examples in addition to her possibly fictional account of what happened at Lysanger. Although it is obvious that Solness doubts the truthfulness of that account, and remembers nothing of their "romantic" interlude, she tells Herdal, in his presence: "Mr. Solness—has such a miraculous memory. All the least little details he remembers instantly" (325). This is the "reality" she would "will" into existence. She reshapes the past by omission, as it were, when she deliberately conceals from Solness the fact that his wife mourns not her children but her dolls (365). And there is her adamant refusal to accept he fact the heights have ever made Solness dizzy, notwithstanding his testimony and Aline's. Consider also the following passages, from the second and third acts respectively. In the first passage Hilde speaks of separation from her father as a painful sacrifice, justified only by her interest in Solness; in the second passage she characterizes her home as a "cage" which she willingly fled:

Hilde (with a quivering of the lips). … it was no such simple matter to leave Father—I am so awfully fond of him. … I think I shall never go home again.

Solness. Never? Then why did you leave him?

Hilde (half-seriously, half-banteringly). Have you forgotten that the ten years are up?

Solness. Nonsense. Was something wrong at home then?

Hilde (quite seriously). It was this impulse within me that urged and goaded me to come—and lured and drew me on as well. (349)

……………………………………………………………

Solness. … Had you a cosy, happy home—up there with your father, Hilde?

Hilde (without stirring, answers as if half asleep). I had only a cage.

Solness. And you are determined not to go back to it?

Hilde (as before). The wild bird from the forest never wants to go into the cage … The bird of prey loves to range—(367)

The first citation follows almost immediately after Solness proposes his theory of "helpers and servers," and boasts of his extraordinary ability to influence the wishes and actions of others simply by willing it. Hilde refers to the "impulse within" her that "goaded" and "lured" her towards Solness not only to suggest their profound bond, but also to encourage his illusion of omnipotence, and so make him feel responsible for her infatuation. Only moments later she suggests precisely this: *Hilde*: "Tell me Mr. Solness—are you certain that you have never called me to you? Inwardly, you know?" (351).

The circumstances surrounding the later passage are different, and demand from her a different response. Shortly beforehand, Solness reveals to Hilde the obligation he feels towards his wife because of the deaths of the boys. "She will never get over it—never in this world," he says (365). He also tells her that he cannot endure the sight of Aline for this very reason (364). It is evident to Hilde that Solness thinks his home a prison. The point of her allusion to her own "cage," coming immediately after she indicates her belief one has the right to "set aside" "some one you know" in order to "grasp at your own happiness" (p. 366), is to suggest that Solness abandon his "cage" as she did hers, notwithstanding his obligation to his wife.

Clearly, Hilde distorts or reinvents the past as present interests dictate. It is, accordingly, impossible to know when she is telling the truth, or even if she is aware of the truth. Indeed, *both* of the preceding accounts may be false if, as her straitened circumstances suggest, there was in fact "something wrong at home" and Hilde's departure was involuntary. Her flirtation with Herdal at the mountain station, his persistent interest in her, which she does not discourage, her remarks to Solness about other relationships she has had suggest that Solness may not be the first victim of this "bird of prey" or the last. In this she perhaps resembles Solness himself, another predator who, as Herdal remarks, has "known a good many woman in [his] time" (304).

Solness realizes that Hilde cannot be trusted. He perceives that her "inventions" are self-serving. As we have noted, he repeatedly questions her account of events at Lysanger. But that is not reason for him to reject her. Rather, it is a bond which unites them; for, as we shall observe, they are alike in this respect. In the final act he suggests to her that the whole episode at Lysanger, the promise which, she says, she then exacted from him and which he now may be about to redeem at great risk, was perhaps a phantom born of her desire. But he nonetheless reaffirms her vision; for it is the vision he prefers. He may not have embraced her, as she insists he did, but he "ought to have done it." (358).

Hilde's immersion in her waking dream, and her fear of unyielding reality, explain why she did not write Solness during their ten-year separation. "I was afraid the whole thing might fall to pieces," she says (354). She preferred ignorance, with the freedom it gave one to imagine or "dream" what one wished, to the possible discovery that she had imagined all.

Both Solness and Aline reveal their deepest secrets and innermost longings to this dream-child. Hilde is, in that sense, the offspring of both, brought into being by their craving to seem, and indeed to be, other than they are. By confessing to her and accepting her illusions Aline, and especially Solness, bestow upon her whatever power she has over them and in that respect give her being. Solness, who, she says, promised her a "kingdom," is primarily responsible:

Solness (looking at her with head bowed).	How have you become what you are, Hilde?
Hilde.	How have you made me what I am? (379)

In effect Hilde replaces the children of flesh and blood that Solness and Aline cannot have, and justly so. For the relationship between husband and wife—like all relationships in *The Master Builder*—is grounded in illusion and deceit.

They have nothing but this to pass on to their legitimate offspring, who are, appropriately, poisoned by the milk that should have nourished them. Their rightful heir is Hilde, who can feed upon dreams. For this reason, too, it is fitting that she occupies the empty nursery. As Solness tells her, "We have no child. But now you can be the child here, for the time being" (313).

Hilde is as responsible for the master builder's "transmutation" as he is for hers. The Solness in which Hilde believes does not at first exist. His fascination with this attractive and mysterious young woman permits her to create him. When he accepts her dream as "real" he becomes part of it. Hilde shapes him just as he shapes his dwellings; at the end she can legitimately call him "her" master builder. Her dream briefly transforms an aging, fearful, guarded, loveless, guilt ridden man into the free and loving creature he had always longed to be. The impossible aspirations embodied in the new house, with the tower Solness cannot climb and the nurseries for the children he cannot have, become through her again seemingly possible. Solness owes to her whatever happiness, whatever love, he knows or expects to know. The placing of the wreath is the consummate expression of that love, and the culmination of that happiness. Like all dreams it vanishes upon awakening, which takes the form for Solness of a real, not imaginary, fall from the tower signifying freedom, supremacy, and renewal.

We have noted in our previous analyses that Ibsen does not use the word "devil" casually. Solness clearly believes it significant:

> Oh, there are devils innumerable abroad in the world, Hilde, that one never sees … Good devils and bad devils; light-haired devils and black-haired devils. If only you could always tell whether it is the light or dark ones that have got hold of you! (*Paces about*). Ho-ho! Then it would be simple enough. (349)

The young Hilde, who nearly caused the master builder's death, is called a "little devil" (McFarlane: "One of those little devils in white"). The mature Hilde resembles her in that respect. But Hilde is a most unusual devil. She is *both* a "light-haired devil" *and* a "black-haired devil," or an agent thereof. As "good" or light-haired devil she liberates the prisoner so long confined to his "cage"; as "bad" or black-haired devil she brings retribution and the perpetual captivity of death. Those functions are inseparable. Her dual nature accounts for her dress and, in part, for the time of her return. When she first enters she incongruously wears mountaineering as well as sailors garb signifying that she is a creature of the heights, the region of light, of "harps in the air," *and* of fatal, lightless submarine depths such as we encounter in *The Wild Duck*. She comes as she did ten years earlier just before the autumnal equinox, when light and dark, white and black, are present in equal measure, signifying her duality, the ambiguity of the experience she makes possible, and its inevitable, fatal sequel. In her capacity as good and bad, white and black devil Hilde restores the master-builder's faith in himself. The arrogance or hubris that once caused him to defy God, the supreme "master builder," revives and with it the impulse to again confront the Creator (378); and that leads to his death

Kaja Fosli also perceives—and believes—only what she wishes to. Solness needs Kaja for two reasons: she provides the adoration he must have to convince himself of his own worth (all the more necessary given his failing powers and his wife's hostility); and he thinks that only through her can he keep Ragnar. It is clear that he does not love her. When she offers to make the supreme sacrifice and "break off" her engagement to Ragnar for his sake he protests violently, and very nearly admits that it is Ragnar, not she, whom he needs:

Solness
(flaring up). Break it off? Are you mad? Would you think of breaking it off … *(with a sudden outburst)*. But, deuce take it—how about Ragnar then! It's Ragnar that I —(301).

After Solness signs Ragnar's plans, effectively ending their collaboration, he abruptly terminates all relationship with Kaja without a word of explanation (356). One would expect her to conclude from this that her worst fears were justified. Moreover, Solness now has Hilde, whom he obviously prefers. But even those revelations do not destroy Kaja's dream.

It is clear that Kaja speaks to Ragnar about this incident; for she tells him of his dismissal. That is implied by this exchange between Solness and Ragnar:

Solness. … And now, you go home. We don't require you to-day.
Ragnar. I know you do not require me any more; but today I shall remain. (370)

However, it is evident from Ragnar's subsequent conversation with Hilde that Kaja conceals from him the fact that Solness wants nothing more to do with *her*. She cannot admit it to herself—renounce the dream that has supplanted reality. According to Ragnar she still insists that Solness kept him only to keep her. Until Hilde enlightens him, he assumes that Kaja's relationship with Solness will continue:

Ragnar (laughs in exasperation). Thank him, when he has held me down year after year! … all merely that he might—! … keep [Kaja] with him …

Hilde (threateningly, clenching her hands). That is not true! You are telling falsehoods about him!

Ragnar. I would not believe it either until today—when she said so herself. ... She said he'd taken possession of her mind—her whole mind—centered all her thoughts upon himself alone. She says she can never leave him—that she will remain here, where he is—(371)

Kaja's confession was probably occasioned by Ragnar's insistence that they marry (oft-repeated in the past), and that she leave with him. He now has the approval he needs to build for himself, and so the way is clear. Her refusal to follow her fiancé, notwithstanding her brutal dismissal by Solness, confirms that she, like Hilde, prefers dream to actuality.

She is as reluctant to acknowledge her duplicitous relationship to Ragnar, which serves as her "dirty linen" as it were. "Heavens! What deceitful eyes she has," says Aline, not without cause (356). Kaja professes an interest in Ragnar's career and is anxious for Solness to approve his drawings, responding "*joyfully*" when he indicates he may do so. Yet, for nearly two years she has been unfaithful to her fiancé in thought and perhaps in deed, and is quite willing to perpetuate that deception. She accepts Solness's suggestion that—even should she marry Ragnar—she remain with her husband in his service. "Oh yes," she says, "how lovely that would be, if it could only be managed" (299). She says nothing about, and is apparently unwilling to consider, a possible conflict between her vows of marriage and fidelity to her beloved.

She attributes responsibility for such questionable acts to others. The decision to marry Ragnar, she tells Solness, is not hers: "Ragnar and Uncle say I must. So I suppose I'll have to give in" (299). Nor will she admit to Ragnar that she willingly betrayed him. She was, she implies, compelled to do so by Solness, who had "taken hold of her mind—utterly and completely." This, one must add, does not require us to attribute mysterious "hypnotic" powers to him, or the assistance of "demonic" helpers. "[P]oor Kaja" is easily manipulated. Solness is obviously aware of and obviously exploits this weakness, and probably did so when they first met. Threatened by Ragnar's departure, he instinctively reached out to the girl who could redeem him and who grasped at any indication of interest on the part of this attractive, successful man. His "magical" interpretation relieves him of responsibility and hence of guilt. He merely "thought"; he did not act. As Brian Crow perceptively remarks:

> We realize that Solness's belief that he exercised a mysterious power of the will on Kaja could be only another aspect of his egocentricity and, more specifically, of his

> desperate fear of youth. He cannot see that Kaja came to him without being asked simply because she was understandably immediately infatuated by this older but still handsome and distinguished man, who appeared to be showing an interest in her. He is so obsessed by his need to keep Ragnar that he is led into an absurdly "magical" interpretation of her spontaneous arrival.[12]

Here, too, we note that the dream contains the seeds of its destruction. The ever-present threat of discovery very likely possessed a certain attractive power, generated a certain excitement, which drew the weak willed Kaja—whose life was otherwise prosaic—to the master builder.

Aline Solness also prefers dream to actuality. She is, like Hilde, immature in this respect—one implication of her interest in dolls. The difference is that her dream has been shattered. For this she blames Solness.

Even as an adult she and the dolls "had gone on living together" (362). Through them she was able to imagine herself the loving mother she was not. As Charles R. Lyons notes, "her retreat into fantasy was an escape from the demands of her real function as mother."[13] There were nine dolls (362), corresponding to the nine months of gestation. It was necessary for Aline to imagine, grotesquely, that she could have given birth to these inert creatures. "I carried them under my heart," she says, "like little unborn children" (363).

We learn that the fire that destroyed her ancestral home unhinged her not because it threatened her flesh-and-blood children, but because it also destroyed her dolls and other precious possessions. Nowhere in the play is the confusion of the dreaming and waking state more evident than in this bizarre transference of affection from the living to the inanimate. And nowhere are its pernicious effects more clearly delineated. For it was the nervous collapse which this loss brought about that transformed Aline's milk from life-giving to death-dealing substance.

Like Hilde and Kaja, Aline also rejects the "real" world when it conflicts with her imaginary one. She must think herself the dutiful mother, and so insisted upon feeding her newborn children despite clear evidence that her milk would harm them. Extrapolating a little, but not, I think, without justification, we can see that she probably refused to admit to herself that she should not nurse them. In this she is like Hilde, who resists the reality of Solness's tragic, ugly death for which she is largely responsible, and like Kaja who refuses to admit that Solness has rejected her. Nor, like them, will she accept responsibility for her behavior. She attributes the needless death of the children (she obviously could have employed a wet nurse) to "a dispensation of Providence" for which one should be "thankful" (361).

Her extraordinary reaction to that event—namely her *lack* of concern—becomes clear in this context. The fantasy that centered about the dolls was motivated by her desire to think herself a devoted mother. The dolls were essential for the perpetuation of that fantasy—which had developed long before her marriage (362)—whereas the children were not. It is quite possible, indeed likely, that Aline resented the twins who had supplanted, but could not replace, her precious dolls. If so, she may have unconsciously wished her living children ill, which perhaps affected her milk. The unacknowledged, unconscious, destructive impulse perhaps ruled in this case just as it obviously does in Hilde's with equally tragic results.

We learn from Aline that she carefully concealed her interest in the dolls from Solness, "living" with them only "so long as he did not see it" (363). He is therefore unaware that her illness was caused by the destruction of her possessions, or that she now mourns not her children but her dolls. Nor does she disabuse him. She encourages his illusion that her "gift" was—in his own words—precisely that of "building up children's souls in perfect balance, and in noble and beautiful forms" (343). When Aline speaks to Solness about the fire she stresses not what really mattered to her—the loss of her dolls and property—but the grief caused by the deaths of the twins and the guilt that she feels for her part in it (330).

Although Aline prefers to think herself the dutiful servant of others' and wishes them to regard her as such, her "confession" to Hilde (361–363) reveals her to be a morbidly self-centered woman. If we look a little below the surface, we perceive that she bitterly resents Solness for the success achieved at her expense. Speaking of the event that made his career possible, she says, "everything that was *mine* was burnt" (emphasis added, 361). She refuses to visit what remains of the garden he used for his dwellings because, she tells Hilde, the original is no longer hers. "Fancy, they have parceled it out—and built houses for strangers—people that I don't know. And they can sit and look in upon me from their windows" (360). Resentment motivates her constant attempts to make Solness suffer by emphasizing overtly or covertly his guilt—attempts all the more reprehensible in that they are based upon the deception that she mourns her children.

As in the examples cited, Aline does not express criticism of her husband directly. She dare not; for then her behavior would clearly conflict with the illusory or "dream" self—the dutiful wife and mother—in which she prefers to believe. Still, she is able to make Solness suffer for the wrong she thinks he has done her.

In order to remind him of her pain, she dresses, with one significant exception, always in "*unrelieved black*"—although the deaths of the children occurred some ten years earlier, and her mourning is, in fact, secretly for dolls and possessions. A stage direction tells us she speaks always "*in a plaintive voice*" (300). She refers to her loss whenever she has opportunity. In the second act, speaking of Knut Brovik's illness, she asks, "I wonder if he isn't going to die now as well? … Yes, yes—depend upon it, Halvard, old Brovik is going to die, too. You'll see that he will" (328). She obviously wishes to imply that Solness profited from Brovik's ruin, which led to the illness that will soon cause his death, just as he did from the fire, which occasioned her illness and the deaths of the twins. When Solness suggests that Hilde sleep in the nursery she replies, "Oh yes. There we have room and to spare" (313). Even the luxuriant plants she tends serve her purpose. They necessarily remind Solness of the garden she no longer frequents and of what he believes to be her ruined "talent," her "gift for building."

Although Aline resents her husband's interest in other women she never speaks openly to him about it, yet never misses an opportunity to make him feel guilty because of it. She will not allow him to touch her, and with few exceptions leaves whenever he enters the room. As Solness notes, "as soon as I come she goes away." Her remarks about Kaja invariably refer to his interest in the girl. Thus, for example, her observation that Kaja "was standing at the desk, as she always is—when *I* go through the room" (355). She is equally suspicious of Hilde:

> *Solness.* … You will find that we shall get on far better after this, Aline. Things will be more comfortable. Life will be easier—especially for you.
>
> *Mrs. Solness* (*looks at him*). After this? … Do you mean—because she has come here? (329)

Aline's constant innuendo succeeds in its actual, if not its acknowledged, intent. But she refuses to admit responsibility. She protests when Solness complains that he owes her a "boundless debt." "A debt to me?" she says, "Then you are—ill, after all, Halvard" (332). She is offended when Solness praises Kaja for her good temper and willingness, welcome enough, he asserts, "especially when one isn't spoiled much in that way." "Can you say that, Halvard?" she replies (303).

The hostility which Aline will not, or cannot, acknowledge, but which is nonetheless a primary motivation, accounts for her extraordinary behavior in the final act. At a critical juncture she abandons Solness, citing duty to strangers (374). By any reasonable standard that obligation should not outweigh her duty to a husband she believes in immanent peril. Although aware of the danger should he attempt to climb the tower of their new home she makes no effort to actually restrain him. She leaves him with Hilde, to whom she assigns the task: "And be sure you keep a firm hold on him," she says, I believe you can do it best" (374). Yet Aline knows that Hilde wishes Solness to place the wreath and believes him capable of it. In her presence Hilde tells Solness "It will be splendid to see you so high up once more. …" Hilde asserts that she knows "quite well" heights do not trouble Solness, and that she herself has seen him "on the top of a high church tower." Solness implies that he may again attempt that feat "this evening" (356–357).

Hilde later confirms her wish to see Solness place the wreath. The passage reveals that Herdal as well as Aline has opportunity to perceive this and that Aline discusses her fears for Solness with him—a matter of some importance, as we shall note:

Dr. Herdal.	… is there anything going on here? I got a note from you.
Mrs. Solness (rises).	Yes, there is something I must talk to you about.
Dr. Herdal.	Very well; then perhaps we had better go in. (*To* Hilde.) Still in your mountaineering dress, Miss Wangel?
Hilde (gaily rising).	Yes!—In full uniform! But today I'm not going climbing and breaking my neck. We two will stop quietly below and look on, Doctor.
Dr. Herdal.	What are we to look on at?
Mrs. Solness (softly, in alarm, to Hilde).	Hush, hush—for God's sake! He is coming. Try to get that idea out of his head … There he comes, doctor. Let me have a word with you.
Dr. Herdal.	Is it about him?
Mrs. Solness.	Yes, to be sure it's about him. Do come in. (364)

Hilde reveals her bias at the very moment Aline entrusts Solness to her care:

Mrs. Solness.	Oh Miss Wangle, you can't think how anxious I feel about him.
Hilde.	Is there anything in this to be so terribly frightened about?
Mrs. Solness.	Oh yes, surely you can understand that. Just think, if he were really to do it! If he should take it into his head to climb up the scaffolding!
Hilde (eagerly).	Do you think he will! (373)

Aline has opportunity to perceive that her husband might attempt the hazardous ascent. She is obviously concerned about that possibility. She is aware of Hilde's wish to see him "standing free and high up." Yet she forsakes him, indeed, delivers him into the hands of Hilde.

Of course, she refuses to consciously acknowledge—and is in that sense unaware of—the significance of her action. It is of a piece with her belief that she is the dutiful wife of a husband she profoundly resents. She "screams with terror" when Solness ascends the tower (381). Nonetheless, there is ample precedent for her withdrawal at the moment of crisis. It is the chief example of the hostility that motivates her throughout.

Although in the privacy of her home Aline dresses always in black. to remind Solness (and Herdal) of her constant—albeit fictitious—grief for her dead children, she appears in public "*wrapped in a large, white crepe shawl*" (359) to hide her subterfuge from the world. Her shawl is a fiction concealing a fiction. It appropriately contributes to the death of Solness, which comes about precisely because of the entrapment of the protagonists in a web of illusory dreams. Significantly, the shawl passes from Aline to Herdal before it comes into Hilde's possession. All possess the actual agent of destruction; and that is as it should be. For all are instrumental in the death of the master builder.

Ragnar Brovik and his father, Knut, appear only briefly and are, therefore, more difficult to interpret. We must chiefly rely upon clues supplied by the pattern of the drama as a whole.

Certain facts are clear. Solness destroyed Knut Brovik in order to establish himself. We have the master builder's own word for this: "in my time I have crushed him, trodden him under foot ... I needed room for myself" (352). Brovik's threadbare garb is a constant reminder of the consequences for this once successful architect. Solness wishes to do the same to Ragnar and very nearly succeeds. Both therefore have cause to hate him and obviously do. Although superficially subservient and obliging, they have been secretly plotting to deprive the master builder of a recent commission. Inner workroom as well as outer office are staging areas for deceit.

On the basis of what little evidence we have, it appears likely that father and son are united less by mutual affection than by their common hatred of Solness. Given Knut Brovik's history, it is reasonable to assume that he wants revenge. This probably motivates, in part, his interest in Ragnar's career. Should the son succeed it will almost certainly be as Solness tells Hilde: "If Ragnar Brovik gets his chance, he will strike me to the earth. Crush me—as I crushed his father" (351–352). Solness's realization of his dream required the ruin of theirs. Now they too dream—of success that ruins his.

Knut Brovik asks for the commission on his son's behalf to conceal his own interest. For the same reason, Ragnar asks for it not for himself, but for his father who, he says "is fast growing weaker" and is now at the point of death (344). His request is consistent with other overt expressions of concern for Brovik's well being, all of which give the impression of a dutiful son. We cannot reconcile Ragnar's' professed devotion with his abandonment of Brovik on his deathbed:

Solness (relieved).	Ah, then I suppose your father is better?
Ragnar.	No. … he had a stroke.
Solness.	Why, then, you must go home to him! You must attend to your father! … Go home, Ragnar. Both to him and to [Kaja]. Give me the wreath. …
Ragnar.	I know you do not require me any more; but today I shall remain. (370)

Fear of possible ridicule rather than compassion for Brovik motivates the master builder's advice to Ragnar. Ragnar's choice is dictated by his hatred of Solness. He comes with the wreath that is to crown the spire. Now that he is free to build he must have the satisfaction of personally handing it to Solness, and, convinced that the latter will not dare place it, the pleasure of witnessing his craven defeat. As he later remarks to Hilde, "*spitefully and scornfully*," "He has kept us down so long—now we are going to see him keep quietly down below himself" (380).

His justification for his absence—that Kaja, who, he now perceives, has betrayed him with Solness, attends the dying man—is obviously inadequate. Ragnar's wish to see Solness humiliated clearly outweighs compassion for his dying father. We need only assume that it was always so, that he always valued Brovik chiefly as an ally in his struggle for recognition, to grasp the reason. With his commission secure in his pocket he no longer needs Brovik to intercede for him or to use as an excuse, and so, like Solness, has left him to die as best he can. Another possible motive is resentment for Brovik's lack of "faith and trust" in him, which caused Ragnar to doubt in own worth, contributing to years of unnecessary, despised servitude.

His erstwhile devotion to Kaja is as suspect as hers is to him. In the last act he tells Hilde that he has only just learned of the affair between Kaja and Solness (371–372). But can we believe this?

Kaja's infatuation is obvious enough to Aline. Even Dr. Herdal suspects it. Nor does Aline try to hide her concern. As Herdal says, "one couldn't very well avoid noticing that your wife … is not particularly fond of this Miss Fosli" (303).

The first words exchanged by Kaja and Solness—without preamble or explanation because not needing any—suggest that they habitually remain after Ragnar and Brovik have left for the day. "Are they gone?" Solness says (292). Aline suspects the purpose of these sessions, as we learn from the incident of the fictitious letter (302). Ragnar and Brovik, better aware than Aline of Kaja's movements, would have even more cause to suspect her.

It is significant, too, that Kaja's desk is within earshot of the draughtsmen's office where Brovik and his son work. Brovik has Kaja close the door between the two rooms to insure that his conversation with Solness will not be overheard. As a rule it is open. And Kaja herself has to caution Solness to lower his voice when he speaks to her. "Hush—they can hear you!" she says (293). But one can easily imagine moments when at least one forgot, for neither is an accomplished conspirator:

Solness (vehemently).	Get up! For goodness' sake get up! I think I hear someone! *(He helps her to rise. She staggers over to the desk. Mrs. Solness enters by the door on the right …)*
Mrs. Solness (with a glance at Kaja).	I am afraid I am disturbing you. (300)

Moreover, Kaja admits that her attitude towards Ragnar changed decisively after she met Solness. She tells him that "there is only one person I care for now! One, and one only, in all the world! I shall never care for anyone else!" (299). In conversation with Herdal, Solness dates this change for us, saying that it began when Kaja first came to work for him, that is, two years earlier: "She seemed to drift quite away from him—when once she had come here to me," he says (306). Surely Ragnar must have sensed some difference in Kaja's attitude attributable to association with, and possibly devotion to, Solness. Taking all into account, it is hardly credible that he is altogether unaware of the affair. His protestations of ignorance (371) ring hollow. However, it is consistent with the pattern of the drama that he would suppress this suspicion given sufficient motive. And that exists.

Because he feared Ragnar's ability, Solness strove to convince him he was second rate. Ragnar tells us he very nearly succeeded. "He … made me disbelieve in myself!" he says (371). Elsewhere he says he never knew Solness feared him as a potential rival. It first occurs to him during his conversation with Hilde. "Is it possible," he says, "that all this time he has been afraid of me?" (372). Ragnar probably thought Solness kept him only in order to keep Kaja, but suppressed his suspicions. To do otherwise would have amounted to conscious acknowledgement that he was no better than the man he despised; that he, too, was willing to use others—even those closest to him—to advance his career. As we have noted, his relationship to his father was, in all likelihood, precisely of this sort, suggesting that Ragnar is in fact a nascent "Solness," equally as ruthless, motivated by the same preoccupation with success—at the expense of others if need be. That preoccupation is evident even in minor matters, such as the filial neglect implied by the contrast between the "threadbare" father who wears a "somewhat discoloured white neckcloth" and his "well dressed" son (291).

We learn from Solness that Ragnar planned to leave him and set up for himself before Kaja came to work for him. Her arrival, he says, induced Ragnar to stay. But why should Ragnar stay once aware of the relationship between Solness and Kaja? And how could he not at least suspect it? The difficulty vanishes if we assume that Ragnar—who had abandoned hope that Solness would help him establish himself and was therefore about to leave—thought he might benefit from the master builder's interest in Kaja by having her intercede for him, as she does—probably at his urging—more than once. Solness might then be induced to approve his drawings.

If we accept the preceding analyses, then Kaja, who is unaware of her fiancée's *and* of her employer's true motives, becomes the victim of all-encompassing deceit. Like the other protagonists, she is lost within a maze from which she can never extricate herself.

Even Herdal, who appears only briefly, has his dreams and a double nature—a face he presents to the world and another hidden from view and from himself. They are evident in his relationship to Aline, to Hilde and to Solness. His first conversation with Hilde suggests more than the fatherly interest we might expect from this "elderly" physician, an interest which by her "pleased" response she encourages:

Dr. Herdal (approaching).	But *I* recognize you, my dear young lady—
Hilde (pleased).	Oh is it you that—!
Dr. Herdal.	Of course it is. (*To* Solness) We met at one of the mountain stations this summer. … *(holds up his finger at her)*. And I'm afraid it can't be denied that you flirted a little with us.
Hilde.	Well that was better fun than to sit there knitting stockings with all those old women.
Dr. Herdal (laughs).	There I entirely agree with you. (311)

The doctor's interest is confirmed a little later:

Hilde (going towards [Solness]*).*	Well, now I must ask you to let me stay the night here.
Solness.	I am sure there will be no difficulty about that ... Now I'll just let my wife know—
Dr. Herdal.	Meanwhile I will go and see my patient.
Solness.	Yes, do; and come again later on.
Dr. Herdal (playfully, with a glance at Hilde*).*	Oh, that I will, you may be very certain! *(Laughs.)* (312)

Herdal assumes. that the girl who "flirted" with him in the mountain station reciprocates his interest. It is the "dream" or fantasy of this elderly man. "Yes, yes, Miss Wangel, "You know how to keep a firm hold on a man, when you give your mind to it," he says, obviously referring to himself as well as to Solness, and so conveying his fascination with her to this attractive young woman (379–380).

Herdal's interest in Hilde is matched by his interest in Aline. He is the confidant of this woman with the "blond ringlets," who "dresses with taste" and still "shows traces of bygone beauty" (300). His frequent visits, and his appeal to Solness on her behalf, suggest a strong attachment. He believes that Solness's flirtations have caused his wife great pain; and must be aware that the arrival of Hilde can only increase it. Solness possesses both women, and, as the doctor suspects, Kaja as well. Herdal is aware that they are but a few of the many women who have succumbed to this powerful, attractive, successful man. "I know you have known a good many women in your time," he says (304). The elderly, "stoutish," doctor "with thin light hair," apparently unattached, but obviously not uninterested in forming an attachment, has cause to envy, possibly to resent, the younger, "healthy and vigorous" Solness with "close-cut curly hair" who is, in effect, his rival for the affections of Hilde and Aline. Given the form and subject matter of the drama as a whole, one can reasonably assume that, like Aline's perpetual mourning, the doctor's always-cheerful demeanor (stage directions give him "*a round good-humored face*") is a mask concealing unsavory unconscious impulses, *his* "dirty linen," from self and from others.

The consequences of this become clear in the final act. There we learn that Aline has told Herdal of her fear Solness might attempt to place the wreath himself. She knows that Hilde, who wishes to see him on high, is responsible, and has almost certainly so informed the physician, who, even without that information, has reason to suspect it. Herdal's lengthy conversation with Solness in the first act (302–310) should have led the doctor to conclude that for Solness this was a time of exceptional trial that could provoke unpredictable behavior. Yet, despite those clear indications of instability,

Hilde's obvious wish to see the master builder place the wreath, her conviction that he safely can (communicated to, or evident to, Herdal), and Solness's intimation that he might attempt just this (of which Aline has told Herdal), the physician accepts without question the master builder's observation that he stands "down below" as "on everyday occasions" (which this is clearly not) for a guarantee of safety (379–380) and assures Aline that there is no danger. Hilde will "keep a firm hold on" Solness just as she has on the doctor.

The doctor is of course aware of Aline's preoccupation with "duty" and of her inclination to leave whenever her husband arrives. The knowledge serves him well on this occasion. On the flimsiest of pretexts, namely "duty" to perfect strangers, he urges, indeed, very nearly insists, that Aline abandon her husband to Hilde at this critical, perilous juncture, notwithstanding Aline's fear that there is "nothing [Solness] mightn't think of doing" (373–374); and he abandons Solness himself, departing with Aline (373–374).

Herdal exhibits the same irreconcilable inner conflict noted in the other characters. The physician does not consciously intend harm to the master builder. His training and profession, his self-respect and standing in the community prohibit that. He attempts to prevent the master-builder's fall by calling for silence and stillness (382). But this occurs *after* the ascent, which he has in effect facilitated, when, as he is well aware, it may be too late. Suppressed envy and resentment are apparently determinative. How else are we to explain Herdal's disappearance at this most critical of junctures and his insistence that Aline leave with him? His gold-rimmed spectacles signify not only a defective view of the outer world, but of the inner. Like the other protagonists he does not know, indeed is unwilling to know, himself.

Solness, too, is the antithesis of the man he imagines himself to be. He callously manipulates those who stand in his way. Yet, in the dream world he inhabits, he never consciously or deliberately does wrong. He is always the victim of evil, never responsible for it. The only event for which he takes responsibility, namely the conflagration that destroyed Aline's ancestral home, is one for which, by his own account, he is *not* responsible.

Because Solness so perceives himself, we must disregard his explanations and justifications of his behavior when we evaluate him. He represents himself as long suffering, idealistic, even heroic, and consciously believes this. His actions show him to be otherwise.

Although fully aware of the danger it posed he did nothing to repair the cracked chimney of Aline's ancestral home. To the contrary, he hoped for a fire, risking the lives of wife and children in order to advance his career. He ruined

Knut Brovik for the same reason, and would have ruined Ragnar had Hilde not intervened. He allows Ragnar to think himself without talent all the while fearing and needing him because of his talent. He sends Brovik to his grave thinking his capable son a failure. He crushed many other worthy, aspiring talents who might have challenged his supremacy. They gather at the end, drawn by the prospect of witnessing the master builder's cowardly reluctance to ascend the tower of his new home (380). He encourages Kaja Fosli's belief that he loves her simply in order to keep Ragnar, and brutally dismisses her when she is no longer useful to him. His infidelity torments Aline, yet he hardly bothers to conceal it. His professed ideal is to "build homes for human beings." "Cosy, comfortable, bright homes; where father and mother and the whole troop of children can live in safety and gladness, feeling what a happy thing it is to be alive in the world—and most of all to belong to each other—in great things and in small" (341). Yet he dreads, and, so far as he is able, suppresses the "younger generation" who are to inhabit those dwellings. His calling is to create living space for others. But this supreme egotist, who ten years before dared to challenge the sovereignty of omnipotent God, repeatedly insists there is "room" only for himself. He has good reason to fear retribution from those whose dreams and aspirations he has demolished to further his own, and from the God he has defied.

Even were Solness the greatest of master builders such behavior would be questionable. But Ibsen does not so depict him. As McFarlane observes: "The situation at the opening of the play reveals a measure of creative impotence that contrasts greatly with Solness's reputation as a prolific and successful master builder. … Such work as is done in his office is by the efforts of two men, father and son, whom Solness pitilessly exploits."[14] Downs notes: "The set up of his drawing office—two rooms it seems, in his own house and a staff of two men and a girl—forbids us to picture him as an architect of outstanding eminence, but in the circumstances of a comparatively small community he is obviously much sought after …"[15]

He attributes his success not to extraordinary ability but to "luck," "fortune" and invisible "helpers." Others attribute it to his ruthless suppression of potential rivals. His *inability* to realize or engineer his structures is stressed. A master builder is by definition not qualified. He depends for that upon the *architect* Brovik, who is "exceedingly good at calculating bearing-strains and cubic contents—and all that sort of devilry" (305). When we meet him Solness is in his decline, needing Ragnar and Brovik's help to maintain the illusion of mastery, fearful that the talented Ragnar will supplant him. His decision to retire after Brovik's and Ragnar's departure confirms that dependency (366).

To conceal his actual motives from himself and from others Solness lies repeatedly, all the while asserting and believing he speaks only the truth. It is evident even in small matters. Truth has become for him whatever serves his ends, in particular the need to think well of himself.

His very first words reflect an effort to conceal the true nature of his relationship to Kaja (292–293). Oliver Gerland's comments are interesting in this connection. He perceives Solness as "a man self-consciously enacting an identity he has constructed for himself in the past." "One thinks of … Solness's playing the master builder for the benefit of Ragnar and Brovik in the next room, while secretly courting Kaja."[16] He pretends not to be certain of Kaja's name to conceal from Hilde his previous, illicit relationship with the girl (355). He cynically encourages Kaja's abject devotion simply in order to keep Ragnar. She is an indispensable pawn. He must periodically reassert his mastery; reconfirm her worshipful submission, imperiously directing her movements as if she were his slave:

Solness (… Looks sternly at her).	Kaja! … *(points imperatively to a spot on the floor)*. Come here! At once!
Kaja (hesitatingly).	Yes.
Solness (as before).	Nearer! (298)

After Solness discovers that Ragnar has surreptitiously solicited and been offered his own commission he must make certain that Kaja is on his side. He will need her help in keeping Ragnar. And so he tests her:

Solness (more gently).	Kaja, don't you really care a little bit for Ragnar too?
Kaja.	I cared very much for Ragnar once—before I came here to you. (299)

Once assured of her allegiance, he appeals to her for aid. It leads to a more open expression of "affection," which is obviously an attempt to manipulate the girl and patently false:

Solness.	… If Ragnar leaves me and starts work on his own account, then of course he will need you himself.
Kaja (wringing her hands).	Oh I feel as if I could not be separated from you! It's quite, quite impossible!
Solness.	Then be sure you get those foolish notions out of Ragnar's head. Marry him as much as you please—(alters his

tone.)—I mean—don't let him throw up his good position with me. For then I can keep you too, my dear Kaja. …

Solness (clasps her head with his two hands and whispers). For I cannot get on without you, you see. I must have you with me every single day.

Kaja (in nervous exaltation). My God! My God!

Solness (kisses her hair). Kaja—Kaja! (299–300)

His abrupt and brutal dismissal of Kaja after Brovik's forced and Ragnar's voluntary departure makes it perfectly clear that for him she was simply a means to an end, to be discarded when no longer useful. To that deception we must add his false assurances to Herdal and to Aline that their suspicions of intimacy with Kaja are without foundation.

When questioned by the doctor, Solness says he has let Aline believe in his infidelity as "a sort of … salutary self-torture" (307). He implies that his unusual behavior may be the result of "madness" which, he suggests, both Herdal and Aline suspect, and on account of which Herdal has been observing him.

But we know that Solness is guilty as charged. Whether or not he has actually bedded Kaja is not the issue. She has become his virtual if not his physical mistress. Although Herdal of course denies it, he and Aline suspect an illicit affair and so *have* been observing Solness. His reference to his "madness"—an instance of the egocentric self-pity that qualifies nearly his every act and statement—veils his duplicitous immorality, diverts Herdal, and puts an end to all probing questions. It makes Solness appear to be the one wronged rather than the guilty party, and so deserving of sympathy rather than condemnation. It is both a stratagem to mislead others, and an illusion in which he prefers to believe because it excuses his behavior in his own eyes.

Nonetheless, Solness is mad, not uniquely as he suggests, but as all are in this drama. Like the insane, the protagonists cannot see things as they are. They perceive only what their self-serving, waking dreams permit them to perceive. Solness's craving for omnipotence (evident, for example, in his defiance of God, in his absurd belief that only he should be permitted to build, and in the conviction—which Hilde shares—that one's will determines the course of events), and his refusal to admit responsibility for wrong, are not evidence of pathological aberration, but simply expressions of egotism, more intense, but not different in kind, from the egotism at the root of nearly all behavior in *The Master Builder*. Only Kaja, the "perfect" victim is perhaps exempt. And even she rejects the unpalatable truth that Solness no longer wants her, preferring the egocentric fantasy or dream that she will be permitted to "remain here, where he is" after Ragnar's departure (371). Ibsen's point is that the exaltation of self which the waking dream permits is characteristic of mankind in general, and has been since the biblical Fall, a truth of which the tragic end of the master builder reminds us.

We have noted that Hilde's account of the past is obviously suspect, yet may be genuine. If her account is true, Solness once promised her a mythical "kingdom," which he could not by its very nature provide and obviously had no intention of providing, in exchange for the very real reward of her adolescent kisses. He used her as he used others, and deceived her as he did them. If true, her experience resembles and stands for all of the many wrongs committed by Solness in the past. Thus it is just that she should demand "payment" ("you owe me this kingdom" she says [367]), and that retribution should follow. If her tale is false, Solness becomes the victim of deceit practiced so long that the deceiver himself can no longer clearly distinguish truth from falsehood, in particular falsehood that supports the dream of omnipotence that leads to his death. And that, too, is appropriate.

Whether we accept or reject her account of the past, Hilde's function is clear: through her we are made to witness retribution, the recoil of wrongdoing upon the guilty. To be sure, she is not the only one responsible. Others, whom Solness has also wronged or deceived, are involved. Although Hilde prompts Solness to attempt the ascent, Ragnar hands him the wreath, and, at a crucial juncture, Aline and Herdal forsake him. Still, Hilde's knock initiates the fatal sequence.

In the second act Solness and Aline pretend to talk honestly about the difficulties that beset their marriage. But their conversation is as replete with self-serving deception as any in the drama. I have already discussed certain aspects of Aline's contribution. Here I would like to speak of what Solness has to say.

In the preceding act he tells Hilde "you are the very being I have needed most" (326). Yet, when Aline accuses him of an interest in the girl, of "sitting there thinking about" her he feigns indifference (328). It is obvious to Aline that he is pretending, and as obvious to him that she knows it. He therefore attempts to shift the topic of conversation from what he has done *to* his wife to what he has done *for* her. Again he lies, and again she catches him up. Aline, too, pretends, emphasizing her grief at the loss of their children while really mourning her dolls and possessions. Their conversation perfectly exemplifies the suppressed motives that invariably prevent honest communication in this cosmos:

Mrs. Solness.	That emptiness [in the nurseries] is dreadful …
Solness (closes the portfolio, rises and approaches her).	You will find that we shall get on far better after this, Aline. Things will be more comfortable. Life will be easier—especially for you. …
Mrs. Solness.	Do you mean—because she has come here?
Solness (checking himself).	I mean, of course—when once we have moved into the new house. (329–330)

It was for Aline, he says, that he built the new house. But his interest in her well-being is as illusory as Ragnar's concern for Brovik. Events confirm this. In the first act Herdal tells Solness that his association with Kaja contributes to his wife's illness. "Could you not engage a clerk?" Herdal says. "Suppose, with her delicate health, all this tries her too much?" (304). Solness not only ignores the doctor's plea, but almost immediately begins a much more serious relationship with Hilde, whom he obviously does not need to retain the Broviks. Indeed, he suggests that Hilde live with him and Aline in the "new house" built supposedly for Aline's benefit, where Hilde will reign as "princess."

As for his apparent concern about the effects of the fire upon his wife, we must not forget that he did not hesitate to parcel out her beloved estate *after* he had opportunity to observe her suffering. He concludes the conversation with Aline with the greatest falsehood of all: "I have never done you any wrong—not wittingly and willfully, at any rate. …" (332). Although, as in this instance, he does not hesitate to lie when it serves his purpose, consistent with his compulsion to think well of himself he bridles at once when Hilde suggests that he "lie" about Ragnar, that is write something flattering on the drawings, which of course would be to tell the truth (352).

His assertion of innocence reveals a second significant aspect of the master builder's character already noted briefly and witnessed in others. Although he is ruthlessly self-serving, lies repeatedly, and manipulates others unconscionably, he will not accept responsibility for wrongdoing. Because he will not, he cannot understand why he feels guilty, indeed, craves as well as fears punishment. His preoccupation with retribution seems to him possible evidence of "madness." In his own estimation, he is always the victim, never the guilty one. As we have noted, he regards his own suffering—actually the consequence of well-deserved guilt—as *undeserved*, a "sort of … salutary torture in allowing Aline to do [him] an injustice" (307).

Solness assumes Aline mourns her children. His guilt and suffering are, then, the consequence of long-practiced deception by a wife whom he thinks he knows but does not. Like the new house, they are the product of belief in illusion. Those emotions are, nonetheless, warranted by wrongs he has actually done Aline, which he denies or seeks to obfuscate. Downs notes "a gnawing remorse about a guilt which actually is no gilt."[17] And that is in part true. Solness professes gilt about events for which he believes he is not responsible in order to suppress consciousness of those wrongs for which he is clearly responsible.

Just as he refuses to accept responsibility for his wife's unhappiness—arguing for example that the conflagration that destroyed her ancestral home did not start where he expected or hoped—so he will not concede that he has knowingly wronged Kaja. He attributes her infatuation—which, as we have seen, he deliberately encourages when it serves him—not to any *conscious* attempt to control her, but to a mysterious emanation of his will, which overruled hers and drew her to him. "I merely stood and looked at her—and kept on wishing intently that I could have her here," he tells Herdal. The next day, he says, she appeared "and behaved as if I had made an arrangement with her" (306). In fact, as we have observed, Solness, who needed Kaya to retain Ragnar, must, indirectly if not directly, have made his wishes known to her. When he accidentally nearly admits to Herdal that he has deliberately and callously seduced Kaya in order to keep Ragnar he interrupts himself at once:

> *Solness.* … Here I have to go on day after day pretending I [love Kaja]—And it's a shame to treat her so, too, poor girl. *(Vehemently.)* But I cannot do anything else! For if she runs away from me—then Ragnar will be off too. (307)

Solness tells Hilde that it was "simply and solely by that fire that [he] was enabled to build homes for human beings …" The fire, the deaths of his children, and his wife's illness were, he says, "The price, Hilde! The terrible price I had to pay for the opportunity" (341). He continues:

> And every single day I have to look on [McFarlane: "I have to stand by and watch"] while the price is paid for me anew. Over again, and over again—and over again for ever!

Hilde (getting up and looking fixedly at him). Now I can see that you are thinking of—of her.
Solness. Yes, mainly of Aline … (342–343)

Solness regards himself not as the guilty party, responsible for the sufferings of others'—which he surely is—but as an anguished bystander "looking on" or "standing by" while "the price is paid *for* [him] anew" (emphasis added). The sufferings of others, and his suffering on their behalf, are necessary if he is to erect the "cosy homes" which those he has ruined, or would ruin, are to inhabit.

This illusion, fantasy or waking dream permits him to think well of himself, despite all evidence to the contrary. To support it he argues that human destiny is shaped by what he calls "trolls," "helpers," and "servers" (347–49). They are actually responsible for the misfortunes that have made his success possible. He has called them, to be sure, but they, not he, are the agents of destruction. He has *done* nothing wrong, but simply *wished* for certain things. Thus he tells Hilde, "It is not one's self alone that can do such great things. Oh no—the helpers and the servers—they must do their part, too, if it is to be of any good. But they never come of themselves. One has to call upon them very persistently—inwardly, you understand" (347). It is "the helpers and servers [who] keep on flaying pieces of skin off other people in order to close [his] sore" (348).

Much of the responsibility for evil is thus shifted to those mythical beings. Solness now only has to absolve himself of responsibility for summoning them in the first place. And he soon does:

Solness (eagerly). There we have it! There we have it, Hilde! There is a troll in you, too, as in me. For it's the troll in one, you see—it is that that calls to the powers outside us. And then you must give in—whether you will or no. (349)

He blames not himself for his wife's anguish, but the trolls and their counterparts, the devils who have taken possession of him. "Yes, these devils," he says to Hilde, "And the troll within me as well—they have drawn all the life-blood out of her. *(Laughs in desperation.)* They did it for my happiness! Yes, yes! *(Sadly.)* And now she is dead—for my sake. And I'm chained alive to a dead woman. *(In wild anguish.)* I—I who cannot live without joy in life" (366). This display of self-pity—completely at variance with the facts in one as calculating and callous as Solness—is obviously aimed at Hilde, whose sympathy, affection and body he seeks. She is to supply the "joy" he cannot live without. Hilde abets and encourages Solness in this, accepting his dream or fiction just as he does hers.

Solness ultimately attributes to God responsibility for the suffering of those who have paid for his success, thus absolving himself completely. It was God "who gave the troll in [him] leave to lord it, just as it pleased. He who bade [the devils] be at hand, to serve [him] day and night." God "made the old house burn down …" and so was responsible for the deaths of the children. "He wanted to give me the chance of becoming an accomplished master in my own sphere—so that I might build all the more glorious churches for him …" (375–76).

But in fact the fire occurred *after* Solness decided to build for self rather than for God. He *wanted* "the old house [to] burn down" so that he could erect domestic dwellings on the spot, and thus "force [his] way upward as a builder" (346). And that was the consequence. "As a builder the fire was the making of me," he says (339, 340). "[T]hanks to the fire I laid out almost the whole of the garden in villa lots; and there I was able to build after my own heart. So I came to the front in a rush" (340).

Clearly, in thought, if not in deed, Solness had abandoned God well before the egocentric gesture of defiance at Lysanger. That confrontation confirmed a previous choice. He had *already* decided to be "a free builder" of domestic dwellings in his own "sphere" (377).

Solness, however, falsely attributes his rebellion not to this prior decision, but to the deaths of the children that followed: "From the day I lost them I had no heart for building churches" (340). His explanation or justification—which assumes that God, not he, was responsible for those deaths and is therefore no longer deserving of his devotion—is not only self-serving but suspect, given the fact that he was willing to risk the safety of those very children for the sake of building "after [his] own heart."

It is clear from his neglect of the defective flue that Solness made no effort to seek out and correct *any* of the hazards of the ancient dwelling. Had he done so, he might have discovered and rectified the problems in the closet where the fire actually started. To that extent he *was* responsible for the fire. He wished for it and so took no steps to prevent it. By attributing the fire and its consequence not to his deliberate negligence but to God's desire that he build only for Him, and by emphasizing that the fire did not break out where he hoped and expected, Solness is able to absolve himself of responsibility, *and* represent himself to Hilde as one uniquely favored by divinity: "one of the chosen people who have been endowed with the power and faculty of desiring a thing, willing a thing—so persistently and so—so inexorably—that at last it has to happen" (347). His illusory version of events has him heroically defying the selfish deity responsible for his tragedy, the deity who allowed the "servers" "helpers" "devils," and "trolls" to prevail. Presenting and believing himself the possessor of special powers, yet ultimately innocent of the misfortunes those powers occasion, he is able to justify inwardly and to others the ruthless manipulation of those for whom he would build "cozy and happy homes." His self-deceptions, evasions and wrongdoing in turn provoke unconscious guilt and conscious suffering for which he characteristically blames not himself but God!

Suppressed guilt for actual, not imaginary, misdeeds, evident as just fear of "retribution," threatens always to become manifest and overwhelm Solness. It is the necessary consequence of his manifold, egregious wrongs. His complex stratagems—his belief in ministers, servers, trolls, devils, and divine intervention—cannot entirely contain that danger. Solness is tormented, inwardly divided, notwithstanding his Herculean attempts to shift the blame for wrongdoing elsewhere. Unlike Hilde, who is almost entirely immersed in her waking dream of grandeur, he bestrides two worlds—that of reality, and that of the dream, each of which is in conflict with and threatens always to annihilate the other. Although his attribution of his sufferings to mythical entities is a self-deluding fiction, his agony is indisputably genuine.

Guilt that cannot be completely suppressed, and almost certainly an unconscious wish to be punished for wrongdoing, underlie the "boundless, immeasurable debt" which he feels he owes Aline. Immersion in a fictional "reality" in an attempt to assuage or suppress that guilt explains his desire to build a new house—complete with nurseries—for a wife who can no longer bear children (the fever that accompanied the fire left Aline barren)—on the very spot where the old house once stood. The nurseries deny by their existence that the tragedy to which Solness contributed ever happened. They assert that children will follow, although it is now impossible. Built "Right above the great quarry" (337), the new house signifies Solness's desire for a "firm foundation," and his belief in the pretense that such a foundation exists. If as Lyons suggests, we read his fear of heights and of falling as manifestations of unacknowledged guilt we can perceive that the tower of the new dwelling expresses an unconscious wish to be rid of guilt. It also, paradoxically, expresses the craving for supremacy which occasioned that guilt. And it affords insight into Hilde's hold over him. Through her he will perhaps acquire the "robust conscience" that will make him truly indifferent to the consequences of his actions, and so once again be able to climb without fear.

However regarded, the new house stands as a monument to the master builder's self-deceit and its disastrous consequences. An essential aspect of the design of the drama is the tension established between the attempt to bury and forget one's wrongs—as the new house was to obliterate the memory of the old—and the recoil of those wrongs, first manifest as Ragnar's "rebellion," subsequently as Hilde's knock, and finally as the master builder's fall from the tower of the new house itself.

Like Hilde, Solness is wonderfully skilled at building "castles in the air"—fantasies about his god-like influence over people and events, about servers, ministers and the like. Those "edifices" are clearly without "firm foundation." His occupation is to materialize the dreams of others,' embody them in wood, stone or steel. In his own life that relationship is inverted. Reality is "dematerialized," supplanted by dream or wishful thinking.

Indeed, the new house itself—where, he assures Aline, they will both be happier—is a fictitious affirmation of his faith in a marriage he has helped destroy. The house rests upon, is "supported" by, two monstrous lies—Aline's pretense that she grieves for her lost children, and Solness's pretense that he is devoted to his wife. It clearly lacks a "firm foundation." The master builder's refusal to build for people he does not know, and Aline's resentment of "strangers" are profoundly ironic, given that they do not and cannot know themselves or each other.

Like Hilde, Solness dreams of falling. And, like her, his dream springs from the fear that the insubstantial scaffold of illusion he has so carefully wrought might someday collapse. In his case, guilt and fear of just retribution which brings with it the desire for just punishment, also contribute to the dream. His dread of heights is psychologically, spiritually, and symbolically appropriate.

The master builder's egotism suggests to him the innovation of transferring the tower from the church, the dwelling place of God, to the home, the dwelling place of man. He renounces God in favor of self. Indeed, he asserts that he is very nearly the equal of God, independent and god-like in his own "sphere": "Hear me now, Thou Mighty One! From this day forward I will be a free builder—I, too, in my sphere—just as thou in thine" (377). The original title of the drama, *Bygmester Solness*, or "Master Builder *Solness*," emphasizes the folly of this arrogant confrontation with the Architect of the cosmos. Solness is decidedly a lesser master-builder, a mere individual. His fall is the inevitable outcome of hubris. "Solness's fall from the tower is as obviously symbolic as Phaeton's fall from the chariot of the sun" writes Shaw.[18] And that is very near the truth. For both were motivated by the universal wish to reach beyond one's grasp.

The parallel with the biblical Fall is clear. Solness falls as those who defied God fell. His tragic end illustrates Ibsen's major thesis: the egocentric waking dream is both our blessing and our curse. Lacking it we can achieve nothing; possessing it we can lose all. To convey this message it was necessary to invent a Hilde who is both creator and destroyer.

Hilde calls the kingdom they will rule together "Orangia." In the original the word is "Appelsinia," "appelsin" meaning "orange" (318). The orange often represents the Forbidden Fruit in religious art, and it surely does here.[19] By encouraging Solness's dream of superiority Hilde offers that Fruit. In effect, she invites him to join her in the kingdom of those who have rebelled against God, a rebellion which Solness himself perhaps initiated at Lysanger. Her role is that of temptress or surrogate Eve. She fosters the master builder's dream of omnipotence, his belief that he is guiltless and superior to others and his reputation and life secure, that—in short—he can climb without fear of falling. He in turn accepts her account of the past, although doubting it, and so supports *her* dream, in which she is to reign as his "princess." The two dreams interact ever more completely and reinforce each other ever more emphatically as the drama progresses. At the end, they coalesce, constituting one dream of a "castle in the air" "with a firm foundation" that Solness and Hilde together have "constructed" and will together inhabit. Solness is perhaps for the first time truly happy. The aging, fearful master builder believes that through Hilde he can regain the love, freedom, and ability to stand on high once his.

That, however, is a fiction destined to succumb to hard, unyielding reality. Hilde's imaginary future with Solness is clearly a fantasy without "firm foundation," a "castle in the air" only. As noted above, the master builder refuses to decisively renounce Kaja. We have her word that she will not abandon Solness even though discharged from his service. Solness justly feels responsible for the deaths of the children and so will remain indebted to Aline, whatever he may or may not learn about his wife's obsession with her dolls. One cannot imagine a blissful future for this "princess," certainly not one commensurate with her waking dream of supremacy. Bruce Bigley points out that "Hilde seems to reject the probability of becoming Solness's mistress by sending him up the tower. It is rather the possibility to fulfill her role as devil, light or dark, the sense of fulfillment which belongs to a muse or siren."[20] If Hilde is to possess the master builder absolutely, if she is to triumph over her rivals completely, it cannot be in this world. Their relationship must end when Solness ascends the tower and places the wreath. He has to die. Only thus can Hilde realize her dream, which is only a dream, an insubstantial "castle in the air." Given her nearly complete immersion in the fiction that she "shall have her castle" (379), her recognition of its impossibility and the attendant death wish are necessarily suppressed, unconscious. However, they undoubtedly contribute to the impulsive, fatal gesture that ends with the triumphant, possessive cry of "*my*, *my* master builder!"

Ibsen's stage directions specify that "*planks and fragments of wood*" fall with the master builder. This detail suggests that his fall is at least partly the result of defective construction. Construed symbolically it confirms the inherent weakness of the new home and tower, the result of the manifold lies and impossible aspirations incorporated into their "structure," and the dire consequences of the master builder's ignorance of the elements necessary for a genuinely "firm foundation." The "castle in the air" he promised Hilde they would erect upon such a foundation as the "one possible dwelling place for human happiness" (377) was always destined to collapse.

Although Hilde is primarily responsible for the master builder's death it is clear that she refuses to acknowledge her critical role or its tragic consequence. As we have observed, Ibsen's other personae also perceive actuality as they would have it, rather than as it is. All deceive themselves and others to accomplish this. In brief, all make the ego or self the touchstone of reality.

That pervasive motif indicates that Ibsen does not want us to regard his play as a study in the abnormal psychology of a few. He wishes to point out, rather, that we resemble his protagonists in our weaknesses, that it has always been thus since mankind's Fall, and that it will continue so indefinitely. Ibsen is quite thorough. He even has Herdal refer to Aline's *former* home as the "grim old robber's castle" of one who obviously preferred himself before others (309). As for the future, it is clear that Ragnar is as ruthless and ambitious as Solness, and will in turn become another such "master builder." To quote Lyons, "The bringing to earth, the crushing of the master builder, is the triumph of Ragnar, the future master builder."[21]

The master builder's desire to build "cosy and happy" homes must be evaluated in this larger context. It, too, rests upon the shifting sands of impossible aspirations and dreams. Such a home must be based upon the "firm foundation" of mutual trust and truth; and these do not exist in the universe of *The Master Builder*. Solness appears to perceive something of the sort shortly before his death.

He knows that the death of Brovik, and the departure of Ragnar, who will replace and surpass him, spell the end of his career. He will build no more, and must justify this fact to Hilde. His remarks are undoubtedly self-serving, and in that respect characteristic; nonetheless they ring true. The dysfunctional marriage of Solness and Aline, the result of his own dream of supremacy that required the destruction of her dream or fantasy; Kaja, who has betrayed her fiancée for the sake of her impossible dream of union with Solness; Ragnar, ruthless and self-serving when it suits him, who nurses his own dream of supremacy, and whose relationship with Kaja has been ruined by her dream; smiling Herdal who dreams or imagines that Aline and Hilde reciprocate his desire; enigmatic Hilde, who, pursuant to her dream, deliberately sets out to destroy what remains of the master builder's marriage—represent humanity in this drama. And so we must agree with Solness's pessimistic assessment:

> ... now I see it. Men have no use for these homes of theirs—to be happy in. And I should not have had any use for such a home, if I had had one. *(With a quiet, bitter laugh.)* See, that is the upshot of the whole affair, however far back I look. Nothing really built; nor anything sacrificed for the chance of building. Nothing, nothing! the whole is nothing! (377)

Ibsen's use of offstage events, which we must reconstruct as best we can, contributes to the ambiguity of the whole, and to the elusiveness of all but these somber truths. The chief instance is the death of Solness. Its significance depends upon his thoughts and feelings as he ascends the tower and at the moment of death; and those—save for the dream that unites Hilde and Solness—are hidden from us. Solness's acquaintance with Hilde is very brief. Of her past he knows only what she has revealed, and that is little enough. Neither he nor we can say positively whether her account of the past is truthful or her expectations what they appear to be. Solness certainly questions both. Does he at the end think her honest and her devotion to him genuine? If not, we can perhaps regard his death as a gesture of heroic defiance prompted by dedication to a dream in which he no longer believes but *would* believe, and so invest a meaningless world of "Nothing" with arbitrary meaning. If her account and commitment are genuine and he thinks them genuine, he becomes the egotist who attempts the impossible task of realizing their complementary dreams of supremacy. If they are ersatz and he thinks them genuine, he becomes an unwitting victim who sacrifices his life for a lie. What were the master-builder's thoughts at the moment when Hilde, for whom he had ventured all, distracted him—deliberately as it must have seemed to him? His "collision" with ugly, adamantine reality perhaps *preceded* his fall.

Solness ends as Adam ended, as the drama in effect asserts all must end who worship self. He falls to his death from the monument to his ego and embodiment of his grandiose dream of supremacy, victim of a fatal infatuation inspired by one who encouraged that dream, an infatuation that briefly gave meaning and direction to his life and ended it. Ewbank's assessment is to the point: "[Solness] is both the mangled corpse at the quarry bottom and the man who got right to the top of the spire. His end, then, is both the defeat and the triumph of the human spirit. We are given the perception (which this play shares with all great tragedy) of simultaneous victory and ruin."[22] As we have observed, that paradox is at the heart of this drama. Lacking his egocentric dreams of supremacy man is nothing. Yet those very dreams destroy the dreamer.

Ibsen's stage directions for the last act specify "*low tumble-down cottages*" [McFarlane: "*mean dilapidated cottages*"] just beyond the "*old wooden fence*" defining the current limits of the master builder's garden (359). They are surely the very structures Solness erected after the hoped-for fire liberated that part of Aline's estate. We must assume that he looks towards them when he delivers his final pessimistic assessment of his career. Their current, neglected state confirms his belief that nothing of enduring significance was "built" after all, that he was a failure in his profession as in his life. The association of structure and personhood throughout this drama suggests that those hovels reflect the spiritually impoverished, insignificant lives of their inhabitants, who, one must assume, are not less self-serving or self-deluding than Ibsen's protagonists. It was for these structures and those inhabitants that Solness sacrificed love, family, and fellowship. The shabby, decaying dwellings perhaps assert that even the heroic act of defiance, the attempt to impart meaning to the otherwise meaningless, may have but transient significance in the cosmos of *The Master Builder*—that, indeed, "the whole is nothing."

Notes

1. Brian Downs, *A Study of Six Plays by Ibsen*, 182.
2. Brian Downs, *A Study of Six Plays by Ibsen*, 188.
3. Brian Downs, *A Study of Six Plays by Ibsen*, ch. VI, section VIII.
4. Address to a Students, Torchlight Procession in Oslo, 22 March 1898 in *Oxford Ibsen* vol. VII, 534.
5. T. S. Eliot, *Selected Essays 1917–1932*, 247.
6. Hermann J. Weigand, *Modern Ibsen*, ch. IX.
7. Charles R. Lyons, *The Divided Consciousness*, 126.
8. Charles R. Lyons, *The Divided Consciousness*, 125.
9. Hermann J. Weigand, *Modern Ibsen*, 291 ff.
10. Brian Downs, *A Study of Six Plays by Ibsen*, 201 fn 4.
11. James McFarlane in McFarlane, *Henrik Ibsen: A Critical Anthology*, 428.

12. Brian Crow, "Romantic Ambivalence," 206.
13. Charles R. Lyons, *The Divided Consciousness*, 129.
14. James McFarlane, in McFarlane, *Henrik Ibsen: A Critical Anthology*, HI, 425.
15. Brian Downs, *A Study of Six Plays by Ibsen*, 179–180.
16. Oliver Gerland in Lyons, *Critical Essays* 234–235.
17. Brian Downs, *A Study of Six Plays by Ibsen*, 202.
18. George Bernard Shaw in Lyons, *Critical Essays*, 31.
19. George Ferguson, *Signs and Symbols in Christian Art*, 35.
20. Bruce Bigley, "Praxis and Stasis," 206.
21. Charles R. Lyons, *The Divided Consciousness*, 133.
22. Inga-Stina Ewbank, "Ibsen's Dramatic Language as a Link between his 'Realism' and His 'Symbolism'" in Lyons, *Critical Essays*, 73.

References

All parenthetical page citations in this text are from *Eleven Plays of Henrik Ibsen*, ed. B. A. Cerf, D. S. Klopfer. New York: *The Modern Library*, 1935. Translators not given but those of plays discussed in this volume appear to be R. Farquharson Sharp (*Ghosts*, *An Enemy of the People*), Edmund Gosse and William Archer (*The Master Builder*, *Hedda Gabler*), and William Archer (*The Wild Duck*). I found those older translations satisfactory for my purposes. In the few cases where translation appeared to be an issue I have appended parallel citations from *The Oxford Ibsen* (*Ibsen* (McFarlane, James Walter, ed. and trans. *The Oxford Ibsen*, 8 vols. London: Oxford University Press, 1962).

Bigley, Bruce. "Praxis and Stasis in Ibsen's 'Bygmester Solness'—or Whatever Happened to Plot and Character?" *Scandinavian Studies* 50, no. 2, (Spring 1978): 195–210.

Crow, Brian. "Romantic Ambivalence in 'The Master Builder.'" *Studies in Romanticism* 20, no. 2 (Summer 1981): 202–223.

Downs, Brian W. *A Study of Six Plays by Ibsen*. Cambridge England: Cambridge University Press, 1950.

Eliot, T. S. *Selected Essays 1917–1932*. New York: Harcourt, Brace and Co., 1932.

Ferguson, George, ed. *Signs and Symbols in Christian Art*. Hesperides Book. New York: Oxford University Press, 1961.

Lyons, Charles R. *Henrik Ibsen: The Divided Consciousness*. Carbondale IL: Southern Illinois University Press, 1972.

Lyons, Charles R., ed. *Critical Essays on Henrik Ibsen*. Boston: G. K. Hall & Co., 1987.

McFarlane, James, ed. *Henrik Ibsen: A Critical Anthology*. Harmondsworth, Middlesex, England: Penguin Books, 1970.

McFarlane, James, ed. *The Oxford Ibsen* v. VII. New York: Oxford University Press, 1966.

Weigand, Hermann J. *The Modern Ibsen*. New York: Henry Holt & Co., 1925.

SELECT BIBLIOGRAPHY

Translations

Archer, William, ed. *Ibsen's Prose Dramas*. New York: Scribner and Welford, 1890.
Ellis-Fermor, Una. *The Master Builder and Other Plays*. Baltimore: Penguin Books, 1958.
Fjelde, Rolf. *Ibsen: The Complete Major Prose Plays*. New York: Farrar, Straus and Giroux, 1978.
McFarlane, James Walter, ed. and trans. *The Oxford Ibsen*, 8 vols. London: Oxford University Press, 1962.
Meyer, Michael, trans. *The Plays of Ibsen*. New York: Washington Square Press, 1986.

Bibliographies

Firkins, Ina Ten Eyck. *The Project Gutenberg e-Book: Henrik Ibsen*, 2006. [e-Book 17719].
Tedford, Ingrid. *Ibsen Bibliography 1928–1957*. Olso: Oslo University Press, 1961.

Speeches and Letters

Speeches and New Letters, translated by Arne Kildal. Boston: R. G. Badger, 1910.
Sprinchorn, Evert, ed. *Ibsen: Letters and Speeches*. New York: Hill and Wang, 1964.

Biographies

Koht, Halvdan. *The Life of Ibsen*. Translated by Einar Haugen and A. E. Santainiello. 2nd ed. Rev. New York: Benjamin Blom, 1971.

Meyer, Michael. *Ibsen, a Biography*. Garden City, New York: Doubleday, 1971.

General Studies

Bentley, Eric. *In Search of Theater*. New York: Atheneum, 1975.

Bentley, Eric. *The Life of the Drama*. New York: Applause Theatre Books, 1991.

Bentley, Eric. *The Modern Theatre: A Study of Dramatists and the Drama*. London: R. Hale, 1948.

Beyad, Maryam, and Mahsa Moradpour. "Ibsen's *The Wild Duck* and Chekhov's *The Seagull*: Classical Tragedy in Modern Perspectives." *Pazhuhesh-e Zabanha-ye Khareji* 49, Special Issue, English (Winter 2009): 5–22.

Bigley, Bruce. "Praxis and Stasis in Ibsen's 'Bygmester Solness'—or Whatever Happened to Plot and Character?" *Scandinavian Studies* 50, no. 2, (Spring 1978): 195–210.

Binding, Paul. *With Vine-Leaves in His Hair: The Role of the Artist in Ibsen's Plays*. Norwich, England: Novik Press, 2006.

Bradbrook, Muriel Clara. *Ibsen, the Norwegian: A Revaluation*. Hamden, Connecticut: Archon Books, 1966.

Brown, Russell. "Taking Ghosts to the Doctor." *Tijdschrift Voor Skandinavistiek* 13, no.1 (1992): 91–103.

Brown, Spencer. "Ibsen Reconsidered." *The Sewanee Review* 88, no.1 (Winter 1980): 144–149.

Brustein, Robert. "Ibsen and Revolt." *The Tulane Review* 7, no. 1 (Autumn 1962): 113–154.

Brustein, Robert Sanford. *The Theatre of Revolt: An Approach to the Modern Drama*. Boston: Little, Brown, 1964.

Calderwood, James L. "*The Master Builder* and the Failure of Symbolic Success." *Modern Drama* 27, no. 4 (Winter 1984): 616–636.

Chamberlain, John S. *Ibsen: The Open Vision*. London: Athlone Press, 1982.

Croce, Benedetto. *European Literature in the Nineteenth Century*. Translated from the Italian by Douglas Ainslie. New York: Haskell House, 1967.

Crow, Brian. "Romantic Ambivalence in 'The Master Builder.'" *Studies in Romanticism* 20, no. 2 (Summer 1981): 202–223.

Downs, Brian W. *A Study of Six Plays by Ibsen*. Cambridge, England: Cambridge University Press, 1950.

Downs, Brian. *Ibsen: The Intellectual Background*. Cambridge: Cambridge University Press, 1946.

Durbach, Errol. *A Doll's House: Ibsen's Myth of Transformation*. Boston: Twayne Publishers, 1991.

Durbach, Errol. *Ibsen the Romantic: Analogues of Paradise in the Later Plays*. Athens, GA: University of Georgia Press, 1982.

Eliot, T. S. *Selected Essays 1917–1932*. New York: Harcourt, Brace and Co., 1932.

Ferguson, George, ed. *Signs and Symbols in Christian Art*. Hesperides Book. New York: Oxford University Press, 1961.

Fergusson, Francis, *The Idea of a Theatre*: NJ: Princeton University Press, 1949.

Fjelde, Rolf, ed. *Ibsen: A Collection of Critical Essays*. Englewood Cliffs, NJ: Prentice-Hall, 1965.

Ganz, Arthur. "Miracle and Vine Leaves: An Ibsen Play Rewrought." *PMLA* 94, no. 1 (January 1979): 9–21.

Goldman, Michael. *Ibsen: The Dramaturgy of Fear*. New York: Columbia University Press, 1999.

Gosse, Edmund. *Henrik Ibsen*. New York: Charles Scribner's Sons, 1908.

Gray, Ronald. *Ibsen, A Dissenting View: A Study of the Last Twelve Plays*. Cambridge: Cambridge University Press, 1977.

Grene, David. *Reality and the Heroic Pattern: Last Plays of Ibsen, Shakespeare, and Sophocles*. Chicago: University of Chicago Press, 1967.

Haakonsen, Daniel, ed. *Contemporary Approaches to Ibsen*, volumes 1 and 2. Oslo: Universitetsvorlagen, 1975

Haugen, Einar Ingvaid. *Ibsen's Drama: Author to Audience*. Minneapolis: University of Minnesota Press, 1979.

Henn, Thomas Rice. *The Harvest of Tragedy*. London: Methuen, 1956.

Hoenig, Leonard J. "Congenital Neurosyphilis as Portrayed in Henrik Ibsen's *Ghosts*." *Dermanities* 6, no. 1 (October 25, 2009).

Holtan, Orley L. *Mythic Patterns in Ibsen's Last Plays*. Minneapolis: University of Minnesota Press, 1970.

Hornby, Richard. *Patterns in Ibsen's Middle Plays*. Lewisburg: Bucknell University Press, 1981.

Hornby, Richard. *Script into Performance: A Structuralist Approach*. New York: Paragon House-Publishers, 1987.

Jacobs, Elizabeth. "Henrik Ibsen and the Doctrine of Self-Realization." *The Journal of English and Germanic Philology* 38, no. 3 (July 1939): 416–430.

James, Henry. *The Scenic Art: Notes on Acting and the Drama*. New Brunswick: Rutgers University Press, 1948.

James, Henry. *Theatre and Friendship: Some Henry James Letters*. London: J. Cape, 1932.

Johnston, Brian. *Text and Supertext in Ibsen's Drama*. University Park, PA: Pennsylvania State University Press, 1989.

Johnston, Brian. *The Ibsen Cycle: The Design of the Plays from "Pillars of Society" to "When we Dead Awaken."* Boston: Twayne Publishers, 1975.

Joyce, James. *The Critical Writings of James Joyce*, edited by Ellsworth Mason and Richard Ellmann. Ithaka NY: Cornell University Press, 1959.

Leland, Charles. "In Defense of Pastor Manders." *Modern Drama* 21, no. 4 (Winter 1978): 405–420).

Lyons, Charles R., *Henrik Ibsen, The Divided Consciousness*. Carbondale, IL: Southern Illinois University Press, 1972.

Lyons, Charles R., ed. *Critical Essays on Henrik Ibsen*. Boston: G. K. Hall & Co., 1987.

Machiraju, A. F. "Ideals and Victims: Ibsen's Concerns in *Ghosts* and *The Wild Duck*." *Modern Language Review* 87, no. 1 (January 1992): 134–142.

Matos, Timothy Carlo. "Choleric Fictions: Epidemiology, Medical Authority, and *An Enemy of the People*." *Modern Drama* 51, no. 3 (Fall 2008): 353–368.

McFarlane, James Walter. *Ibsen and Meaning: Studies, Essays and Prefaces, 1953–87*. Norwich, England: Norvik Press, 1989.

McFarlane, James Walter. *Ibsen and the Temper of Norwegian Literature*. Oxford: Oxford University Press, 1960.

McFarlane, James Walter, ed. *Discussions of Henrik Ibsen*. Boston: Heath, 1962.

McFarlane, James Walter, ed. *Henrik Ibsen: A Critical Anthology*. Harmondsworth, Middlesex, England: Penguin Books, 1970.

McFarlane, James Walter, ed. *The Cambridge Companion to Ibsen*. Cambridge: Cambridge University Press, 1994.

McFarlane, James Walter, trans. *Henrik Ibsen: An Enemy of the People, The Wild Duck, Rosmerholm. Oxford World's Classics*. Oxford, England: Oxford University Press, 1999.

McFarlane, James Walter, and Jens Arup, trans. *Henrik Ibsen: Four Major Plays. Oxford World's Classics*. Oxford, England: Oxford University Press, 2008.

Moi, Toril. "Hedda's Silences: Beauty and Despair in *Hedda Gabler*." *Modern Drama* 56, no. 4 (Winter 2013): 434–456.

Moi, Toril. "'It was as if he meant something different from what he said—all the time': Language, Metaphysics and the Everyday in *The Wild Duck*." *New Literary History* 33, no. 4 (Autumn 2002): 655–686.

Moi, Toril. *Henrik Ibsen and the Birth of Modernism: Art, Theater, Philosophy*. New York: Oxford University Press, 2006.

Mueller, Janel M. "Ibsen's Wild Duck." *Modern Drama* 11, no. 4 (Winter 1968): 347–355.

Nicholson, Mervyn. "L'Homme Fatal in *Hedda Gabler*." *Modern Drama* 35, no. 3 (Fall 1992): 365–377.

Nordau, Max. *Degeneration*. New York: Appleton, 1912.

Northam, John. *Ibsen: A Critical Study*. Cambridge: University Press, 1973.

Northam, John. *Ibsen's Dramatic Method: A Study of the Prose Dramas*. London: Faber and Faber, 1953.

Olsen, Stein Haugom. "Why Does Hedda Gabler Marry Jørgen Tesman?" *Modern Drama* 28, no. 4 (Winter 1985): 591–610.

Østerud, Erik. *Theatrical and Narrative Space: Studies in Ibsen, Strindberg and J. P. Jacobsen*: Aarhus: Aarhus University Press, 1997.

Peacock, Ronald. *The Art of the Drama*. London: Routledge and K Paul, 1957.

Peacock, Ronald. *The Poet in the Theatre*. New York: Harcourt, Brace and Co., 1946.

Robins, Elizabeth. *Ibsen and the Actress*. New York: Haskell House, 1973.

Robinson, Michael, ed. *Turning the Century: Centennial Essays on Ibsen*. Norwich: Norvik Press, 2006.

Shaw, Bernard. *The Quintessence of Ibsenism; Now Completed to the Death of Ibsen*. London: Constable and Co., 1922.

Soloski, Alexis. "'The Great Imitator': Staging Syphilis in *A Doll's House* and *Ghosts*." *Modern Drama* 56, no. 3 (Fall 2013): 287–305.

Sprinchorn, Evert. "The Unspoken Text in *Hedda Gabler*." *Modern Drama* 36, no. 3 (Fall 1993): 353–367.

Templeton, Joan. "Of This Time, of This Place: Mrs. Alving's Ghosts and the Shape of the Tragedy." *PMLA* 101, no. 1 (January 1986): 57–68.

Templeton, Joan. *Ibsen's Women*. Cambridge: Cambridge University Press, 1997.

Van Laan, Thomas F. Generic Complexity in Ibsen's 'An Enemy of the People.'" *Comparative Drama* 20, no. 2 (Summer 1986): 95–114.

Weigand, Hermann J. *The Modern Ibsen*. New York: Henry Holt & Co., 1925.

Williams, Raymond. *Modern Tragedy*. London: Verso Editions, 1979.

Young, Robin. *Time's Disinherited Children: Childhood, Regression, and Sacrifice in the Plays of Henrik Ibsen*. Norwich, England: Norvik Press, 1989.